The RSVP Cycles

By the same author:
CITIES
FREEWAYS
NEW YORK NEW YORK

The RSVP Cycles

Creative Processes
in the Human Environment

Lawrence Halprin

George Braziller, Inc., New York

Published simultaneously in Canada by
Doubleday Canada, Limited.

For information, address the publisher:
George Braziller, Inc.
One Park Avenue
New York, N. Y. 10016

Second printing
Standard Book Number: 0-8076-0557-3
Library of Congress Catalog Card Number: 73-107750

Designed by Barbara Stauffacher Solomon

Printed in the United States of America

This book is dedicated to my wife,
Ann Halprin, to honor many years of
collaborative creativity.

Acknowledgments

I would like here to acknowledge the many people who have assisted me in the development of this book. Often ideas lie smoldering and gestating for years before they erupt, so that what emerges may have no specific attribution. For that reason I would like simply to acknowledge the importance of Walter Gropius,* under whom I studied at Harvard, for my attitudes about creativity, and of Rabbi Max Kadushin who, many years ago, spoke to me of organic thinking. In addition I want to thank all those good friends and colleagues here and abroad with whom I have worked professionally all these years—each one of whom has influenced me profoundly: what I do emerges in great measure from our interactions.

I owe a debt of immeasurable gratitude to my staff, my associates, and all the members of my office past and present, and our workshop participants, for influencing me. My partners, Don Carter, Satoru Nishita, Richard Vignolo, and my associates have not only shouldered extra burdens while I have been "away on this trip" but also have given me the time to work with it. Particular mention should be made of the assistance of Billie Vrtiak for her superb secretarial professionalism, and also Dai Williams, Curtis Schreier, and Norma Leistiko. I want to thank my daughters, Daria, who first pointed out to me that no RSVP cycles were complete without an inner cycle of the self, and Rana, who contributed text and ideas on mystic scores.

Sue Yung Li Ikeda deserves special and major thanks for her unfailing patience, incisive questioning of ideas, and valuable editorial assistance throughout our "trip" with this book.

The following people have read the manuscript and offered comments: Dr. Paul Baum, Lawrence Livingston, Jr., James T. Burns, Jr., Seymour Evans, Leslie Hood, Jerry Rubin, Charles Amirkhanian, Dr. Fritz Perls, and Stewart Udall. I want to thank each one of them for the exciting dialogues we have had together.

Finally, a special thanks to my wife, the dancer and choreographer Ann Halprin, who has discussed with me all the concepts in this book, many of which derive from mutual work and many of which she has led me to explore.

A word about the layout of this book. It was "scored" in a unique way. The various people working on production are separated by three thousand miles of space. Since the editors and the publisher and his production staff are in New York and the author and designer are in San Francisco, the two groups had to find some way to work together allowing each to keep their own creativity but meshing their work together. First, the master score for all the scores was developed by the author. Then graphic designer Barbara Stauffacher Solomon established a module for the page layout and prescribed an unusual system of varying type sizes. The graphic scores and illustrations were laid out by Mrs. Stauffacher Solomon in San Francisco and the rest was completed in New York by Irving Garfield, Production Manager, and the James S. Wilkinson Associates, according to the score set up by the designer.

A final note of thanks to George Braziller and the environmental editor, James T. Burns, Jr., for their constant and creative support.

Lawrence Halprin

Sea Ranch
October, 1969

---

*Early work on scores in relation to performance was explored under Gropius at the Dessau Bauhaus.

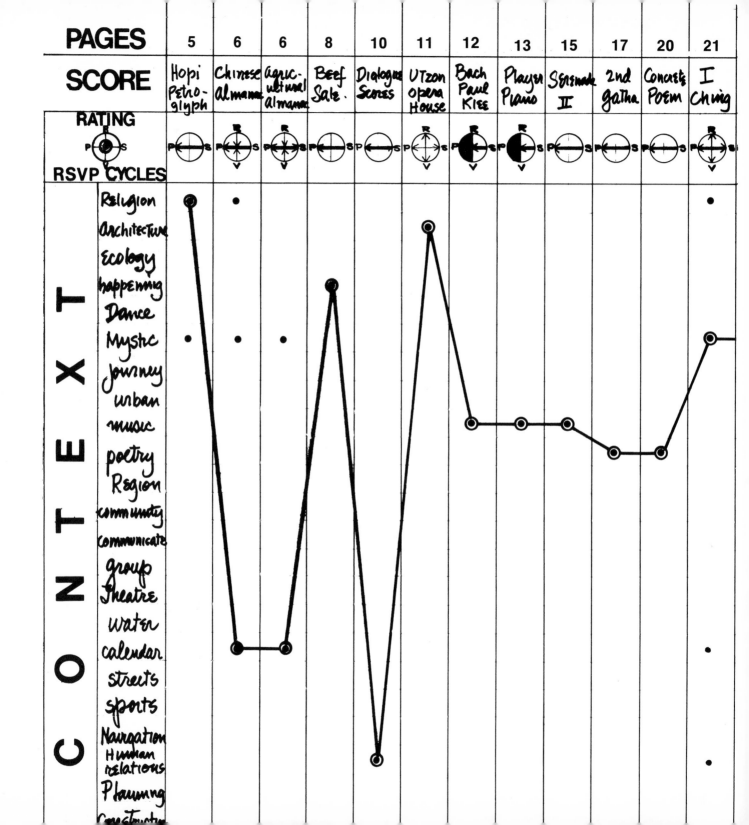

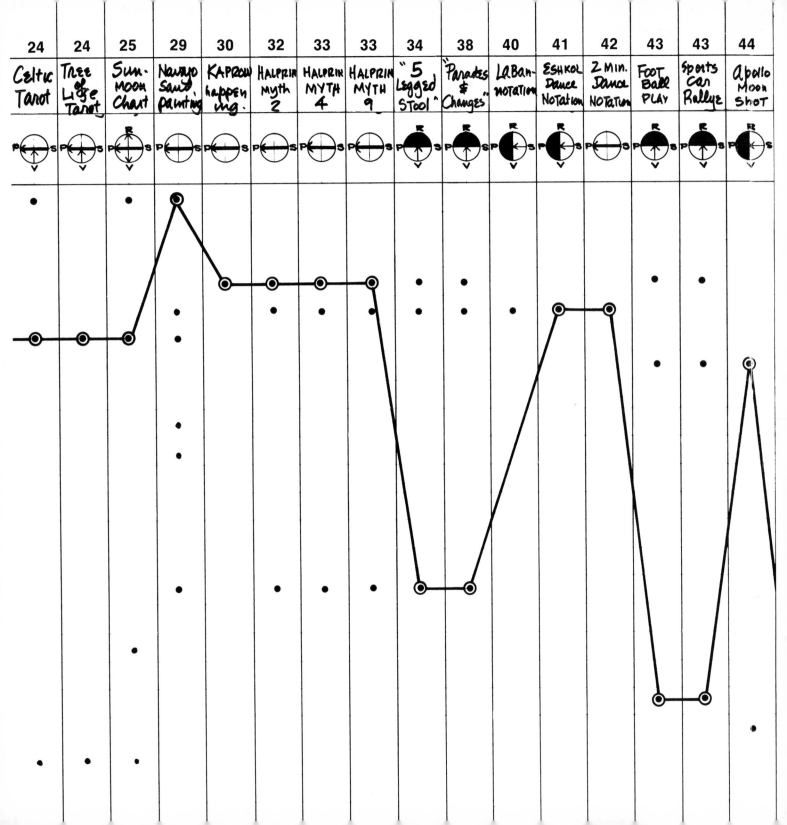

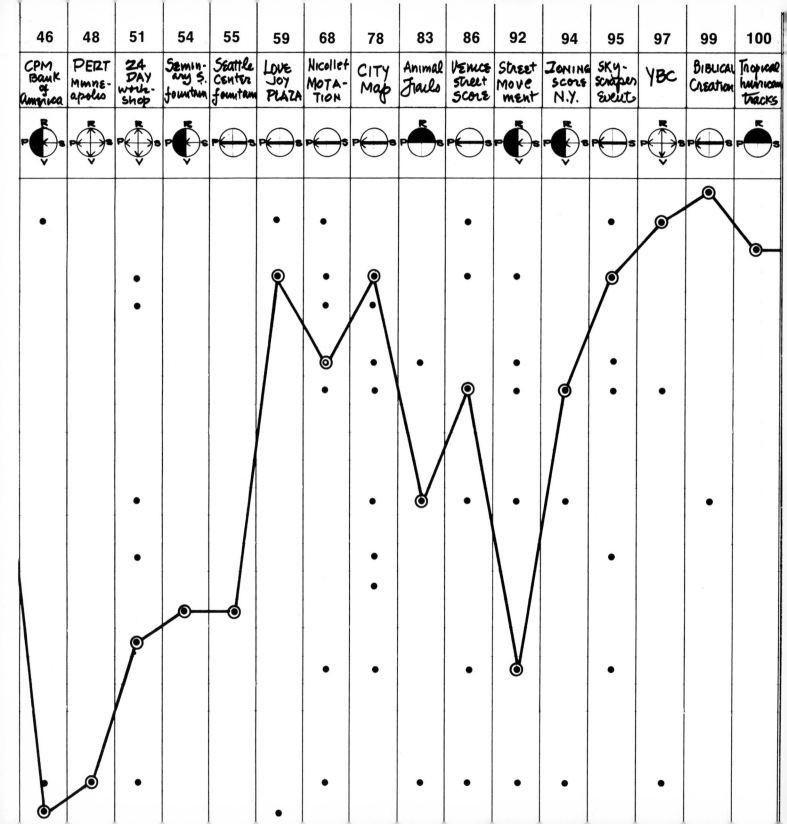

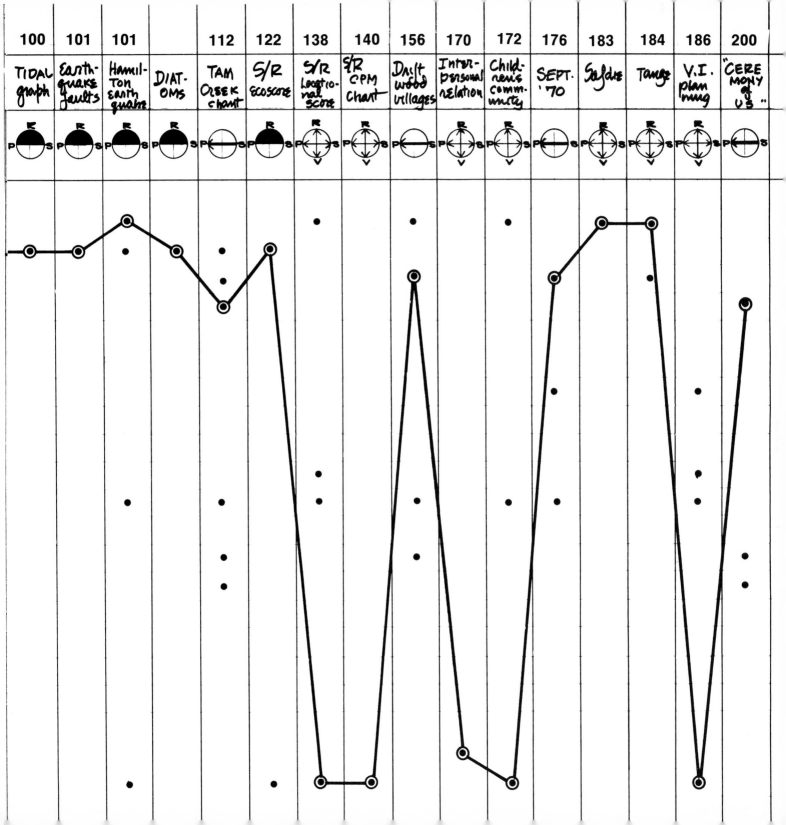

The RSVP Cycles

This book started as an exploration of "scores" and the interrelationships between scoring in the various fields of art. Scores are *symbolizations of processes* which extend over time. The most familiar kind of "score" is a musical one, but I have extended this meaning to include "scores" in all fields of human endeavor. Even a grocery list or a calendar, for example, are scores. I have been interested in the idea of scoring not any one particular system of scoring, but scoring generally—for many years. This interest grew, quite clearly, from two different sources: first, because I am professionally an environmental designer and planner involved in the broad landscape where human beings and nature interface; and, second, because of my close relationship to dance and theatre due largely to my wife, the dancer and choreographer Ann Halprin, who is Director of the Dancers' Workshop in San Francisco.

Both sources—the new theatre-dance and the environment as Ann and I have been practicing them are nonstatic, very closely related in that they are process-oriented, rather than simply result-oriented. Both derive their strengths and fundaments from a deep involvement in activity. In both fields, the process is like an iceberg—9/10 invisible but nonetheless vital to achievement. Both deal with subtleties and nuance, intuition, and fantasy, and go to the root-source of human needs and desires—atavistic ones at that. In both, values, though there are not *really* demonstrable. At all events, I have been searching for years (and still am) for means to describe and evoke processes on other than a

simply random basis. I thought that this would have meaning not only for my field of the environmental arts and dance-theatre, but also for all the *other* arts where the elements of time and activity over time (particularly of numbers of people) would have meaning and usefulness.

I saw scores as a way of describing all such processes in all the arts, of making process visible and thereby designing with process through scores. I saw scores also as a way of communicating these processes over time and space to other people in other places at other moments and as a vehicle to allow many people to enter into the act of creation together, *allowing* for participation, feedback, and communications.

I hope that scores will lead into new ways of designing and planning large-scale environments of regions and large communities whose essential nature is complexity and whose purpose is diversity. I hope that the idea of scores will make it possible to work in these regional communities as a method for energizing processes and people and the natural environment in a constantly evolving and mutually involving procedure over time. I hope to see scores used as catalytic agents for creativity leading to a constructive use of change.

The book itself has been a score. It was not preconceived, and has developed its own shape while a work in progress. I started out with many scores for ephemera that I have done for dance or for environmental events over the years. I explored primitive scores, mystical scores,

scores for happenings, based on my wife's work, and my friends' who, too, have been pushing the boundaries of their arts. Inevitably much of my own personal experience comes out in the "scores for environment" which is my professional interest as well as the field in which I have had my most personal experiences. Thus, the second half of the book explores street scores, ecological scoring, city scores, and finally community scores.

As I worked on the score for the book, however, one fact kept on emerging to plague me—it demanded consideration, and this became increasingly clear as I worked in communiscores. The scheme was not complete. As I worked on "scores" *only,* there were elements that kept cropping up in the creative process which were not being covered by the scoring procedure, especially as the projects became more and more complex. I found that scores are nonjudgmental—this is one of their primary characteristics. Yet, in many instances some outside witnessing must be reached, some selectivity must be exercised. But scores do not do that, they don't perform that function.

As I continued to develop the characteristics of scores, I found that often before actual scoring starts the scorer has a great deal of preliminary work to do in collecting resource material, inventory items to use in his scores. I found too that a clear differentiation has to be made between the score, which is usually graphic and precedes the fact, and the performance, which is the resultant of the score. Much of my own professional life has been involved in this apparent dichotomy: between the score and the performance, which are not the same but have an intricate relationship to each other. Finally, I found that scoring has to allow for feedback, for analysis before, during, and after a score is created in order for the score to develop and allow for change—to grow. All of these important functions were not, I found, taken care of in scores themselves.

In the long run, I found that what I had really been working toward, what I really wanted to explore, was nothing less than the creative process—what energizes it—how it functions—and how its universal aspects can have implications for all our fields. Scores alone were not doing this. I was not interested exclusively in what the score-performance relation was—how the particular event, the building, or piece of music, or piece of legislation, was beautiful, but how the process of arriving at it came about. I found that I had to understand the context in which it all had happened and to see if, by understanding what had been required to make it happen, I could apply the principle across many fields, in a multidimensional way, to a life process. Perhaps most importantly, I found that by themselves scores could not deal with the humanistic aspects of life situations including individual passions, wills, and values. And it seemed necessary to round out the scheme so that human communications—including values and decisions as well as performance—could be accounted

for in the process.

When that became clear, I found that the procedures I needed to get all these inputs into some context had four parts and they were all interrelated. Each part had its own internal significance, but got really cracking only when it related to the others. They have similarities to Jung's cycle which he called the compass of the psyche.

R *Resources* which are what you have to work with. These include human and physical resources *and* their motivation and aims.

S *Scores* which describe the process leading to the performance.

V *Valuaction* which analyzes the results of action and possible selectivity and decisions. The term "valuaction" is one coined to suggest the action-oriented as well as the decision-oriented aspects of V in the cycle.

P *Performance* which is the resultant of scores and is the "style" of the process.

Together I feel that these describe all the procedures inherent in the creative process. They must feed back all along the way, each to the other, and thus make communication possible. In a process-oriented society they must *all* be visible

continuously, in order to work so as to avoid secrecy and the manipulation of people.

Together they form what I have called the RSVP cycles.

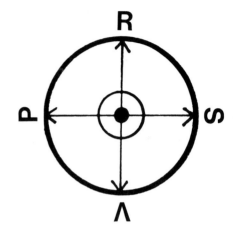

The diagram above describes the multidimensional and moving interconnectedness between all the elements of the cycle. It can as correctly read, P, R, S, V or any other combination. It is important to emphasize this point. The cycle operates in *any* direction and by overlapping. The cycle can start at any point and move in any direction. The sequence is completely variable depending on the situation, the scorer, and the intent. By chance, when I finally put the headings together, they spelled out RSVP, which is a communications idea meaning "respond."

This is, obviously, an essential ingredient of the cycle. As I and others have worked with this cycle it has become increasingly clear that the cycle must work at two levels. The first of these is the personal, private level of the self, which I use with a lower case "s" according to the Gestalt psychology. This cycle is an inner one, appropriately, and refers to one's own personal Gestalt: the people who are close to you, your personal environment, attitudes, interests, even hangups; one's motivational inner world as distinct from one's outer-oriented world. This self RSVP cycle appears graphically at the center of the community or group RSVP cycle which is in effect composed of all the individual self-cycles engaged in the activity of scoring.

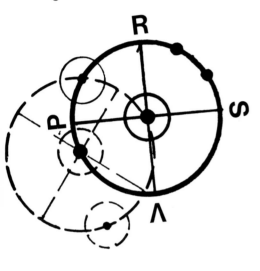

The private, self-oriented inner cycle and the community, group-oriented outer cycle together make up the RSVP cycles necessary to encompass all human creative processes. Thus, this book deals with the two RSVP cycles. The inner cycle as the separate self and the outer cycle as the collective self: individual and community.

The book then, as it finally emerged, describes the effects of the various parts of the RSVP cycles on the process of scoring and on what has emerged from the scores. Particularly in the environmental section the entire RSVP cycles are in use all the way through, since in the planning of environments every facet of the total cycle has importance. In other activities, the whole cycle is not desired or required. When that is the case it has been so indicated. I believe, however, that it is important for anyone working with the cycle to understand where he is concentrating and which parts are operating. If, for instance, you jump immediately to Performance (P), you are improvising. There are times when improvisation, for example, or spontaneous responses are vital to the release of creative energies which might remain locked up otherwise. But these energies can often fruitfully feed back into the rest of the cycle or remain isolated for their own sake. See page 38 for a review of this point.

The same is true of other portions of the cycle, which does not have to be in complete operation at all times in order to have validity. A personal word to my friends in the various art fields. I know how resistant artists are to the notion of "systematizing" the processes by which art evolves. There is a feeling that to enclose gossamer is to destroy it. These RSVP cycles and the point of "scoring" are not meant to categorize or organize, but to free the creative process by making the process *visible*. I have found, in my own work, that my hangups come when there is some buried obstacle that I don't understand and can't flush out. When I can "see" obstacles or get in touch with what's blocking me, I can deal with them. I hope the RSVP cycle can do that; it already has for me and others with whom I have discussed it.

Nothing in the RSVP has attempted to define talent or ability or the final making of a decision which, of course, remains at the very core of personal creation. The magic of magic remains.

For me, professionally, the significance of the RSVP cycles lies in the fact that as an ecological designer I have always been interested in pluralism and the generative force of many contributions to solutions. I view the earth and its life processes as a model for the creative process, where not one but many forces interact with each other with results emergent—not imposed. I see the earth as a vast and intricately interrelated ecosystem. In this system all of the parts have value, and they are all moving toward balance.

The essential characteristic of community in the ecological sense is that all of the parts are functioning within their own habitat, that no one element outweighs the other, that each contributes to the whole. Thus, the total ecological community has the characteristics of an organism which lives and grows and reproduces itself in an on-going process.

Human communities, too, have many of the same characteristics, to which we have given the name *"tout ensemble,"* that is, the sum is itself valuable and has more qualities than simply one additive of its ingredients. Such a *"tout ensemble,"* recently threatened by a freeway in New Orleans, has been saved by the decision not to allow that one factor to undermine the balance of the whole community. The balance of climax communities in natural or human communities is tenuous and easily destroyed—it is not static—it exists as long as no one force outweighs the others. This I believe to be true of all human affairs and a model for all the life processes in which we need to integrate ourselves.

One of the gravest dangers that we experience is the danger of becoming *goal-oriented.* It is a tendency that crops up on every hand and in every field of endeavor. It is a trap which goes like this: things are going poorly (in the realm of politics or religion or building a city or the world community or a personal relationship or whatever). As thinking people we must try to solve this problem that faces us. Let us set ourselves a "goal" upon which we can all agree (most goals after all are quite clearly moralistically based and incontrovertibly "good ideas"). Having set ourselves this goal we can then proceed posthaste to achieve it by the *most direct method possible.* Everyone can put his shoulder to the wheel, and systems engineering, technology, and our leader (or whatever) will get us to the agreed goal.

It doesn't work! The results of this oversimplified approach, now coming into general vogue, are all around us in the chaos of our cities and the confusion of our politics (or other politics—fascism and communism are clear statements of this approach). It generates tension in personal relationships by burying the real problems; it avoids the central issue of education, which is

why today's young people are dropping out; it is destroying the resources and physical beauty of our planet; and it avoids the basic issue.

There are evidences of this kind of thinking in the attempt to make a science out of community design, as if by assigning it the term "science" then the goal of perfection can be reached. Human community planning cannot ever be a science anymore than politics can rightly be called political science. Science implies codification of knowledge and a drive toward perfectibility none of which are possible or even desirable in human affairs. When ekisticians, for example, say that the "search for the ideal is our greatest obligation" they are making the same basic error that all goal-oriented thinking does—a confusion between motivation and process. We can be scientific and precise about gathering data and inventorying resources, but in the multivariable and open scoring process necessary for human lifestyles and attitudes, creativity, inquantifiable attitudes, and openness will always be required. There is a vast difference between being idealistic, which is life-oriented and process-oriented, and utopian, which implies a finite and formal goal. In that sense scores are non-utopian.

We don't really want to be involved in goal-making or goal-solving. Fritz Perls says, "Scores face the possible where goals face the impossible." What we want, what we desperately need, is a feeling of close and creative involvement in processes. It is the *doing* that we all enjoy and which is meaningful to us. That is what is needed in education, in the

ghetto, and in the young and the downtrodden who feel that they are excluded from the process of decision-making in our communities; certainly it is needed in personal relations. It is on-goingness, the process that will build and develop great cities and regions and a world community on this planet Earth. By involvement in process we all interact, our input is significant, visible, meaningful, useful, and no one point of view can hold us in thralldom. Scores are not goal-oriented; they are hope-oriented.

This is why "scores," which describe process, seem to me so significant. It is through them that we can involve ourselves creatively in "doing," from which, in fact, structure emerges—the form of anything is latent in the process. The *score* is the mechanism which allows us *all* to become involved, to make our presence felt. Scores are process-oriented, not thing-oriented. In dance and theatre this works through open scoring, which establishes "lines of action" to which each person contributes and from which a final performance then emerges. In personal relations scoring allows a constant interaction devoid of the moralisms and shoulds and shouldn'ts which inhibit growth and deep contacts and involvements. In the planning of communities a score visible to all the people allows each one of us to respond, to find our own input, to influence *before* the performance is fixed, *before* decisions are made. Scoring makes the process *visible.* For that reason scores seem to me the key link in the entire RSVP cycles—though only one link, still at the core of the whole procedure.

4

The RSVP cycles is a balanced scheme in which all the parts are mutually related and constantly interacting. It functions best when all parts are operating. Its purpose is to make procedures and processes visible, to allow for constant communication and ultimately to insure the diversity and pluralism necessary for change and growth.

Hopi petroglyph from San Cristobal carved as a propitiatory gesture to corn pests.

Planning for future events is the essential purpose of a scoring mechanism. Scores are notations which use symbols to describe processes over a period of time. Scores generally employ graphic symbols but they also may use words, or sounds, either written or spoken—often sung. Scores are devices used for controlling events, of influencing what is to occur. They may also record events from the past (a reconstructed battle plan) or notate what is happening in the present (daily stock-market graphs). But the real importance of a score is its relationship to the future. A score is a way of using media to cause things to happen—to plan, if you will. They are related in Husserls' "intentionality"—they are "orientation-oriented." From earliest times men have striven to control the future through the symbolization inherent in scores. The earliest cave paintings were attempts, through paintings, to insure good luck in hunting. The symbolization of the various deities in *all* religions has been a technique to capture through images and incantations the power of the unknown, and thus influence the course of events.

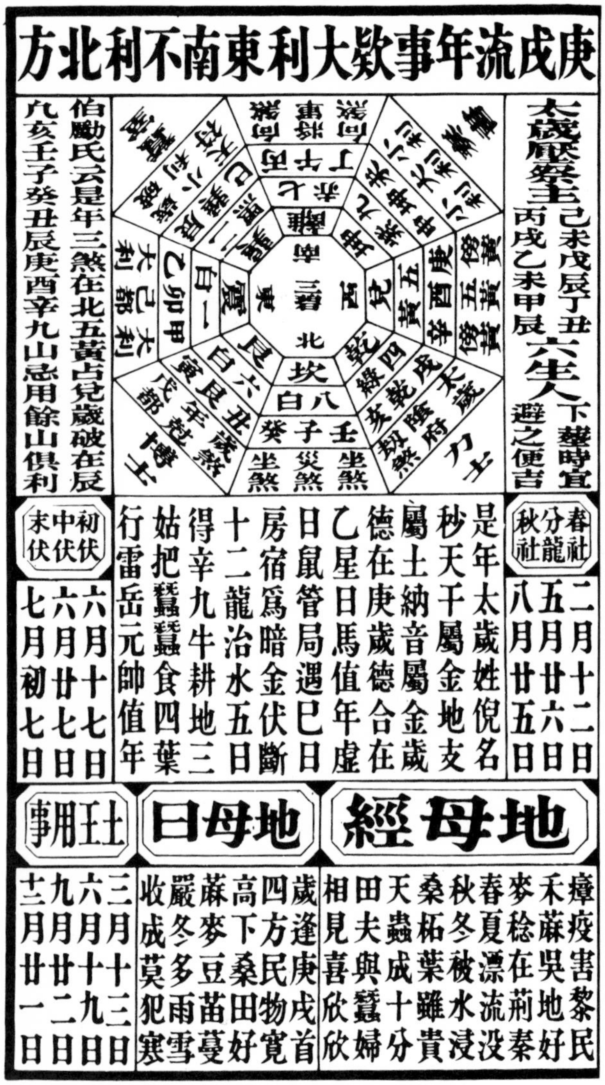
庚戌流年事欵大利東南不利北方
是年太歲姓倪名
秒天干屬金地支
屬土納音屬金歲
德在庚德合在
乙星日值年虛
日鼠管局遇巳日
房宿爲暗金伏斷
十二龍治水五日
得辛九牛耕地三
姑把蠶食四葉
行雷岳元帥值年
春社 分龍 秋社
二月十二日
五月廿六日
八月廿五日
初伏 中伏 末伏
六月十七日
六月廿七日
七月初七日
地母經
地母曰
土王用事
瘴疫害黎民
禾蔴吳地好
麥稔在荊秦
春夏漂流没
秋冬被水浸
桑柘葉雖貴
天蟲成十分
田夫與蠶婦
相見喜欣欣
歲逢庚戌首
四方民物寬
高下桑田好
蘇麥豆苗蔓
嚴冬多雨雪
收成莫犯寒
三月十三日
六月十九日
九月廿二日
十二月廿一日

JUNE, 6th Month

Days and Weeks	Remarkable Days	H. W. h.	The Moon: South morn. h.m.	Place & Age	rises morn. h.m.	Miscellaneous Particulars	The Sun: fast m.	rises h. m.	sets h. m.
Monday	1 Nicodemus	11	9 47	27	2 31	♀ sets 9:44e ☌ ♄ ☽	2	4 33	7 22
Tuesday	2 Marcellus	12	10 39	28	3 03	Castor sets 10:56e.	2	4 33	7 23
Wednesda	3 *Jeff. Davis b.*	1	11 32	29	sets eve.	3. Arcturus so. 9:26e.	2	4 33	7 23
Thursday	4 Darius	2	ev. 27	0	8 32	So. Cross so. 7:30e.	2	4 32	7 24
Friday	5 Boniface	3	1 23	1	9 23	Deneb. so. 3:47 mo. ☌ ♂ ☽	2	4 32	7 25
Saturday	6 Artensius	3	2 15	2	10 04	sets 12-1 mo. Cl. ☌ ♀ ☽	1	4 32	7 25
23]	*2nd Sunday after Trinity*					Day's length 14 hours 55 minutes			
Sunday	7 Lucretia	4	3 06	3	10 39	rises 10-12 eve.	1	4 31	7 26
Monday	8 Medardus	5	3 53	4	11 07	Pollux sets 10:23e.	1	4 31	7 27
Tuesday	9 Barnimus	6	4 36	5	11 31	Moon Apogee	1	4 31	7 27
Wednesda	10 Flavius	6	5 17	6	11 52	Ophiuchus so. 11e.-1 mo.	1	4 30	7 28
Thursday	11 Barnabas	7	5 57	7	morn.	11. Unuk so. 10:22e.	0	4 30	7 28
Friday	12 Basilides	8	6 37	8	12 12	♂ sets 8:36 eve.	0	4 30	7 29
Saturday	13 Tobias	9	7 17	9	12 32	ri. 8-10e. ☌ ♅ ☽	slo.	4 30	7 29
24]	*3rd Sunday after Trinity*					Day's length 15 hours 0 minutes			
Sunday	14 Children's Day Flag Day	10	8 00	10	12 55	Antares so. 10:57e.	0	4 30	7 30
Monday	15 Vitus	10	8 47	11	1 17	Hercules so. 11-12e. ☌ ♃ ☽	0	4 30	7 30
Tuesday	16 Rolandus	11	9 39	12	1 46	Spica so 7:43 eve.	1	4 30	7 30
Wednesda	17 Nicander	12	10 36	13	2 22	N. Crown so. 9:30-10:30e.	1	4 30	7 31
Thursday	18 Arnolphus	1	11 38	14	3 07	Lyre so. 12-1 mo.	1	4 30	7 31
Friday	19 Gervasius	2	morn.	15	rises eve.	19. Sickle sets 11-12e.	1	4 30	7 32
Saturday	20 Sylverius	2	12 42	16	9 11	Bernice's Hair so. 7e.	1	4 31	7 32
25]	*4th Sunday after Trinity*					Day's length 15 hours 1 minute			
Sunday	21 Fathers' Day Summer begins	3	1 46	17	9 53	Sum. beg. ☉ ent. ♋ ☽ Peri	2	4 31	7 32
Monday	22 Achatius	4	2 46	18	10 27	♃ sets 1:07 mo.	2	4 31	7 32
Tuesday	23 Agrippina	5	3 42	19	10 55	Corvus sets 10:30-11:30e. ☊	2	4 31	7 32
Wednesda	24 *John, Bapt.*	6	4 34	20	11 20	Algenib ri. 11:09e.	2	4 32	7 32
Thursday	25 Elogius	6	5 23	21	11 44	25. ri. 9-11e.	3	4 32	7 33
Friday	26 Jeremiah	7	6 09	22	morn.	□ of Pegasus ri. 10-11e.	3	4 32	7 33
Saturday	27 7-Sleepers	8	6 56	23	12 08	Algol rises 11:35e.	3	4 33	7 33
26]	*5th Sunday after Trinity*					Day's length 15 hours 0 minutes			
Sunday	28 Leo	9	7 44	24	12 35	Fomalhaut ri. 12:31 mo.	3	4 33	7 33
Monday	29 *Peter & Paul*	10	8 34	25	1 05	so. 7:30-9:30e. ☌ ♄ ☽	3	4 33	7 33
Tuesday	30 Lucina	11	9 26	26	1 40	rises 1:42 mo.	4	4 34	7 33

The purpose of art in primitive societies has been simply as a scoring mechanism, a functional purpose by which earlier societies influenced events. This "primitive" attitude toward the functional purposes of art as a tool for influencing events extends to modern times. The uses to which dictatorships put art must be understood in this same light. It is not so much that they foist representational art on their artists, but that they envision art as a specific kind of tool—a specific kind of scoring device to be used to "control" events. They see art now, as did primitive societies, as a way of influencing the course of events in directions decided upon by the rulers of the society. Hierarchically controlled societies have closed attitudes about art, because they view art as a closed score to influence events in the interest of their own self-image. But primitive scores were not only the provenance of art and artists, they also were part of the early purposes of law, religion, of the hunt, and of the rhythms of agriculture and farming.

A page from the Chinese almanac forecasting the "run" of the coming year. The top line predicts that the east-south direction will be auspicious and north unfavorable. Within the octagon are the compass directions with south facing the top of the page. The lower part indicates seasonal changes and their relationship to agriculture.

A comparable page from a farmer's almanac for the sixth month of 1970.

There are many different kinds of scores, many systems of scoring, many kinds of things and events that scores record. The real nub of the issue, however, is what you control through the score and what you leave to chance; what the score determines and what it leaves indeterminate; how much is conveyed of the artist-planner's own intention of what is to happen and to what degree what actually happens and the quality of what actually happens is left open to chance; the influences of the passage of time; the variables of unforeseen or unforeseeable events; and to the feedback process which initiates a new score.

The essential quality of a score is that it is a system of symbols which can convey, or guide, or control (as you wish), the interactions between elements such as space, time, rhythm, and sequences, people and their activities and the combinations which result from them. Not all scores invoke all of these elements—scores vary as to what they can or are intended to control. The characteristics of the type of score as a potential controlling or communicative device is a function of the particular art form and its inherent limitations. It also has a great deal to do with the attitudes and intentions of the scoring artist. Scores have been a means of recording past events, of prognosticating the future, and of influencing the present. Scores extend over time and space to communicate and control; they have involved myths and rituals, mysticism and religion. They have been used to record folklore and communicate music to future generations. For centuries scores have been used to plan cities and build buildings, to write plays and diagram procedures.

Scores have enabled us to reach out to other people, even across cultural and language barriers, and tell them what we would like to have happen. Scores have made it possible, as well, for us to say to someone else what happened to us.

Plans from which buildings are built are scores.
Music is composed and recorded by scores.
Mathematics is a score.
Concrete poems are scores.
Stage directions for a play is a score, as is the written dialogue itself.
A shopping list is a score.
A football play is a score.
The choreography of dance can be determined by a score.
Navajo sand paintings are scores.
The intricacies of urban street systems are scores as are the plans for transportation systems and the configurations of regions.
Construction diagrams of engineers are scores.
$E = MC^2$ is a score.

8

The different elements that scores deal with vary considerably with the art form and the field of work.

Scores are ways of symbolizing reality—of communicating experience through devices other than the experience itself. The score of a musical event is not itself music anymore than the plan and the elevation of a building *are* the building. But the one predates the other and in our complex society is required by the other. First comes the score and then the performance. But they are inextricably interrelated.

Increasingly the difference between scores as communication mechanisms and controlling devices becomes significant.

Some scores are used to *control* events with precision—some scores are simply communicative devices—others do both or combinations of each. Here are some examples of elements that scores engage in:

Space   Present
Time   Future

Sound	Past (recording a
Smell	previous experience)
Touch	Configuration
Sequence	Cost
Event	Precision
Rhythm	Form
Movement	Force
Action	Locale
Gesture	People
Interaction	Light
	Natural configurations

These elements, put together in a variety of ways, produce the work of art—some are controlled and some can be left undetermined as part of the designer's choice. When the work emerges in its final form it will possess qualities resulting from both the controlled and noncontrolled elements, and the work will have its own unique characteristics.

In the following chart are a few examples of different scores and an analysis of to what degree, as intended by the designer as an element of the scoring technique, they control or leave open.

	CONTROL	ENERGIZE	HOW MUCH
Words	X	X	depends on use
CPM chart	X		with great precision
I Ching		X	mystic (open to personal interpretation)
Tarot		X	mystic (open to personal interpretation)
Paintings		X	per intent of artist
Zoning	X		varies with laws, etc.
Football plays	X		feedback during the play
City Plans	X		change over time
Music	X (classical)	X (new)	varies with intent of the musician
Poetry		X	varies with intent of the poet
Evaluative listening	X		gives advice
Active listening		X	feeling and understanding of listener
Movement	X	X	varies with intent of choreographer
Beef sale		X	activity of many ladies

Scores can either control or allow leeway. The difference, however, is enormous. In the older music, scoring devices were used to control, with precision, the notes and true intervals played by the performer. A Bach score is Bach and not something else. It communicates exactly what Bach had in mind and controls what the performer does. The newer musical scores on the other hand are not devices for control in the same way, they communicate an idea and a quality—what emerges is something both more and less than what was intended. The hand of the composer lies less heavily on the performer.

In the field of architecture the reverse sequence is true—plans, as scores, were originally used to guide and communicate an image of what the building was to be, but the participating craftsmen exercised a great deal of latitude in their own choices and contributions to earlier buildings. There was much greater allowable latitude for individual participation and creativity. Today, building workers are simply technicians; all is precise and prefixed, not only form and proportion but performance standards and repetitively prefabricated units are joined together according to preordained scoring devices. Tolerances are minimal, and mechanical, electrical, as well as

structural elements all must dovetail together with great precision. The modern building emerges not in response to the immediate contribution of thousands of workers but as a predetermined event planned years in advance and simply assembled to match the intent. The score controls absolutely, with assembly-line logic.

Fortunately, this closed and controlled approach is not necessarily inevitable and there are techniques by which the architectural score can be freed from rigidity to permit a freedom in the emergent form of building as well as the acceptance of the interaction of time, the necessities of chance and change, and the input of many people. See page 94.

In fields of human interaction scores can be used to control or communicate, depending on their intention and purposes. Words seen as scoring devices can score for interaction and mutual feedback or they can order and thus block interaction—preventing communication. Vast new areas of understanding and communication among people open up when this relation is understood—when the word as a scoring device becomes a generator of feedback between people rather than an ordering or injunctive mechanism.

Score for dialogue between people.

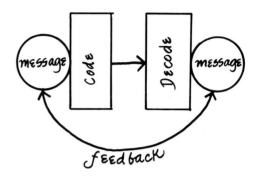

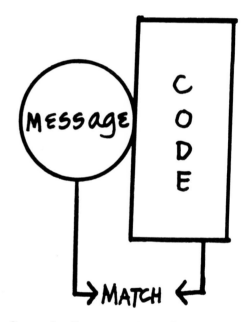

Score for "congruent sending."

One of the common problems in communications between people is that the listener prejudges the content of the message rather than attempting to understand the "feelings" behind the message, *i.e.*, Valuaction (V) in the cycle is operating to the exclusion of the score itself. New understandings of how "active listening procedures" and "congruent sending messages" can "open up" dialogues are at the core of the new view of words as communicative rather than controlling devices. (Based on a theory by Dr. Thomas Gordon, Psychologist.)

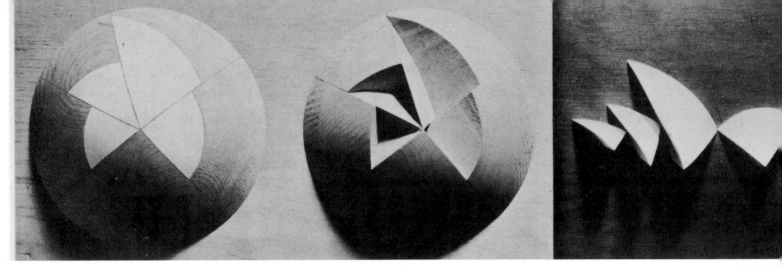

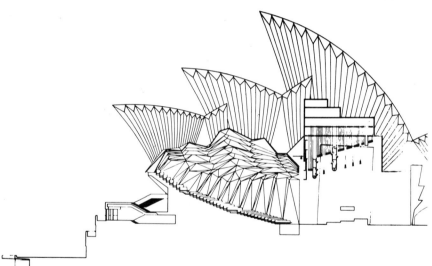

The Sydney opera house by Jorn Utzon—an intricate architectural masterpiece which had to be scored through other than standard techniques by cutting out segments of a wooden ball. This is in Utzon's words, "done as easily as slicing up an orange."

The most significant discovery we have made in modern scoring is the influence of the scoring device itself on the resulting product. We have begun to realize that, to a considerable extent, the technique of scoring controls what happens. John Cage was asked: "When you compose do you think notation first or sound first, may I ask?" "Yes, you may ask. Both constitute inseparable entities, I cannot separate them." The established scoring techniques determine what the limits of the art form can be. In classic musical scoring for example, notes and time intervals are established as are pitch and time. Even the quality is established (by words) and the performers' positions are absolutely fixed in space on stage. This kind of score in itself controls the character and quality of the resulting composition and fixes a limit beyond which music, as an environmental event with feedback, cannot go. Except for some limited passages where improvisation is called for, traditional music leaves little latitude except "interpretation" to the performer. Today's new musicians have had to develop their own form of scoring in order to break through to a new kind of music. Traditional music notation simply precluded the kind of music they wished to compose. When we attempt to design architecture through accepted techniques of plan and elevation the resulting form of buildings is severely limited by our graphic inability to draw, and thus communicate, certain kinds of intricate forms. Thus, real intricacy of forms is limited by the standard architectural scoring devices.

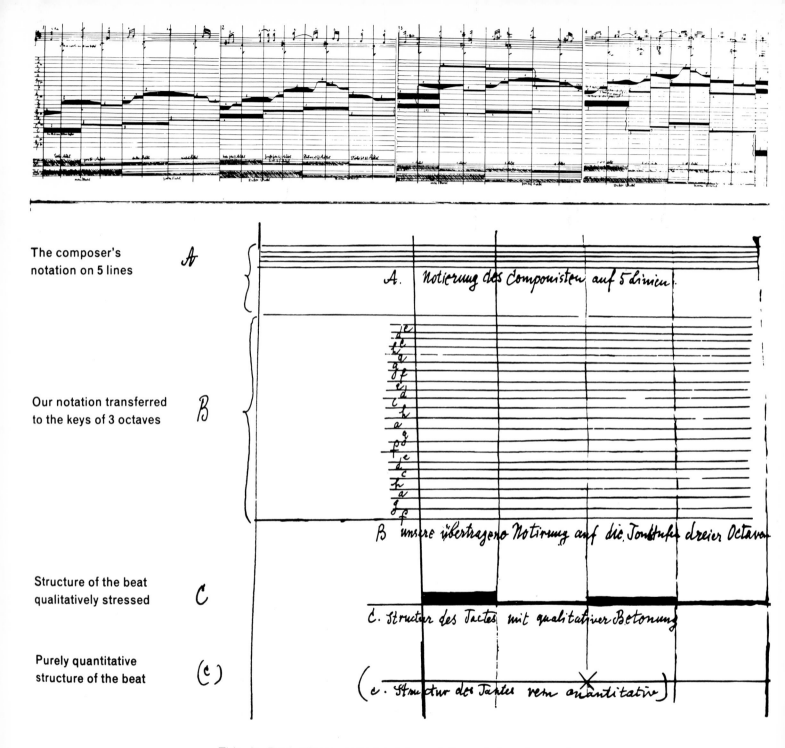

The composer's notation on 5 lines — A

Our notation transferred to the keys of 3 octaves — B

Structure of the beat qualitatively stressed — C

Purely quantitative structure of the beat — (c)

This is Paul Klee's pictorial interpretation of two bars of a three-part passage by Bach. Bach's notation is at the top.

Words themselves, as communication scoring devices, limit human interaction because of the inherent limitations of verbal systems and people's personal interpretations of the emotive content of words, which can vary widely. It is important to realize how limiting verbal communication is and how much it can control (as a score) or not control what happens. The difference between cultures and age groups and the relationships between words and gesture, even distance between people, as a scoring device has vast implications in the communication of ideas and attitudes. Scoring mechanisms themselves limit results and therefore it is necessary to re-examine the kinds of limits imposed by traditional scores.

The simplest way to describe the new attitudes toward scoring is by a musical passage from Bach, two bars of a three-part movement. The Bach notation is as precise and controlling as he could make it, what was left for the performer was a matter of technique and interpretation. Even Paul Klee's attempt to invest the score with expressive quality by pictorial representation of quality adds one more dimension to a notation which had already fixed all the elements into an established configuration. Two hundred years after the event, the score controls the performer as well as communicating to him what he should do. Bach reaches out over the centuries to our time and prefigures what should happen with intricate precision. Basically no interaction is possible—the performer plays what is there with a greater or lesser degree of talent—he is a technician rather than an artist, a medium not a contributor.

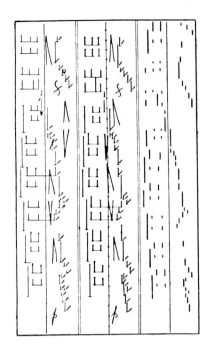

26 *Making a perforated strip. Left: a passage from Chopin's Waltz op. 59 No. 1 (posthumous) recorded on the strip by a pianist. Centre: The strip after corrections have been made—ready for perforation. Right: The perforated strip is ready for reproduction.*

better, was not entirely mechanical. The perforated strips were produced by means of a Morse code recording made during the musician's performance. As he played the piano every key, when touched, set electric current in motion; the electromagnets then affected the recording mechanism according to the force of each note struck. Fundamentally, then, this was simply an improved version of J. F. Unger's recording mechanism. Small errors in the pianist's performance could be corrected. The recording thus obtained served for the manufacture of rolls.

Similar methods were used for the production perforated cards for other automatophonic instruments as well, particularly for the orchestrion. It was which called for considerable skill and precision 'orchestrator', as the man who transferred the music the rolls was called, had first to make a study of composition concerned, particularly if it was an arrangement of an orchestral piece. The prepared pattern printed on strips of cardboard folded like the page book. After the marked places had been perforated card was tested on the instrument for which it intended, so that errors arising during marking or foration could be corrected. This master-card was used for mass production in the same way as the m roll for the pianola. Organs and harmoniums often additional perforated cards to help in controlling registers.

The slightest error in the perforated strip or on cylinder led to faults in the performance which the h ear could easily detect, and so each job had to be c lated at least to a fiftieth of a second. This meant tha pins on the cylinders or the holes in the rolls had t placed exactly to half a millimetre. The effect of atm pheric conditions on the exact parts of the mechan or the result of long use, led to tiny changes w

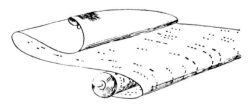

27 *A roll of perforated 'music' for the pi*

The ultimate development of this kind of controlling musical score in which the performer is a medium, is the punched rolls used in player pianos. The rolls are both performer and score.

The score and accompanying directions for a piece by Charles Amirkhanian indicate far less attempt at control and require participation by the players in *forming* the music. What happens has been started and energized by the composer, but the actual music derives from the players themselves.

"Serenade II Janice Wentworth" was scored and performed, 1967–1968, by Ted Greer and Charles Amirkhanian. The scores indicate how the new music has influenced the scoring technique, and the score itself has responded to the requirements of the music as an open environmental event. Charles Amirkhanian comments on his method as follows:

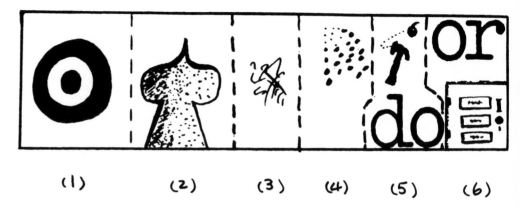

(1)   (2)   (3)   (4)   (5)   (6)

This drawing is a score meant to be "performed" or "executed." However, as is not the case with most notational systems, the performer or performers are not presented with a specific set of code keys for interpreting the notations of each score. Rather, he must approach any one score with a set of attitudes in mind, the components of which I shall now outline.

There is no single way to perform any one of my scores. Each one of them is simply a matrix containing performance stimuli. What we are dealing with, then, is a finished drawing—in itself a "work of art"—which in turn will serve as the stimulus for another work of art, i.e., a performance of music or a play, the making of a painting or a sculpture, the presentation of a series of events, ad infinitum—or preferably, any combination of the foregoing. Contained in each matrix are various visual images. It is from

these images that the artist will derive the individual actions which will constitute a performance.

The composer has developed various major areas in the score. Within each area is a series of images which is intended to evoke responses. The six images shown could affect various artists, for example, in the following ways:

A. As played by a concert musician, specifically a percussionist. (1) strikes gong; (2) plays record of music from Russian Orthodox Mass on portable phonograph; (3) scratches butt end of xylophone sticks jerkily across tympanum head; (4) plays about fifteen notes on xylophone in middle and high registers; (5) utters the word "due"

while raising hammer, and "doe" while smashing a walnut; (6) utters "or . . ." and proceeds to exit by means of the nearest visible door.

B. As performed by a painter as a performance piece, or a finished product, or both. (1) throws ten darts at the blank canvas, puncturing it; (2) squeezes a full tube of white paint onto the surface of the canvas; (3) brushes on ink delicately; (4) paints several of the dart holes a bright red; (5) paints an apple on the canvas— there is a large nail in the apple—the apple is bleeding; (6) wires an oar to the canvas—under the oar is painted the word "door."

C. As realized by a theatrical director, dramatist, or actor. (1) The curtain

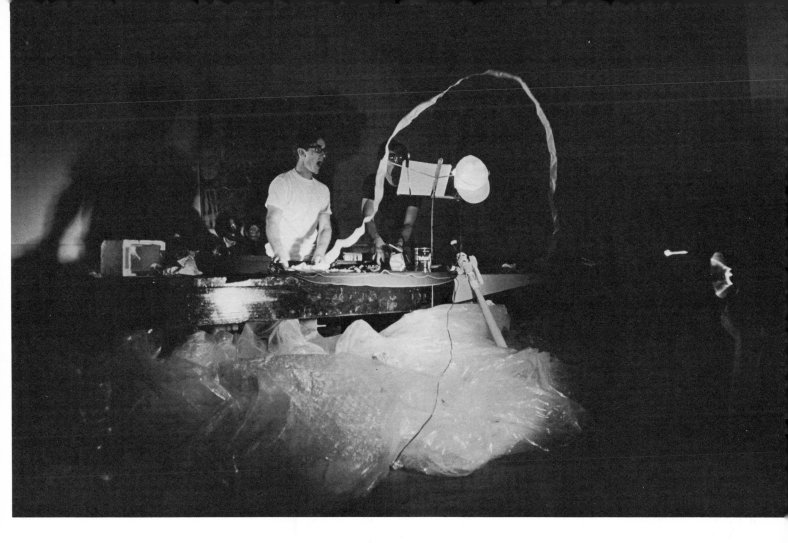

rises; onstage is an enormous plastic eyeball, fifteen feet in diameter, staring straight ahead. (2) A man walks onstage in front of the eye, stops, spreads his legs, raises his hands above his head, and places his palms together. (3) Fifteen seconds later he lowers his arms and shuffles his feet as if attempting to tap dance. (4) He stomps his right foot repeatedly and at various volume levels in mock frustration. (5) He pulls a hammer from his pocket and marches, with his back to the audience, right back to the eye. He knocks once very sharply with the hammer on the pupil of the eye. (6) A door opens in the pupil and he climbs in. The door slams behind him. The curtain falls.

. . . Scores of this nature do not limit themselves to performance only by artists with formidable technical resources; anyone may participate. The only requirement is a willingness to approach a series of nonverbal images with the intent to "read" them with a fluency somewhat akin to our present facility with verbal images. In this regard, here is a new path for introducing art disciplines to "non-artists." The person approaching the score in order to make a painting, for instance, is not taught that only those who can paint recognizable figures, such as torsi and geraniums, can possibly be visual artists. Rather, he is encouraged to paint his responses, since there can be no one "correct" series of responses. He is encouraged further by the sense of purpose which results from adhering to a score.

Charles Amirkhanian,
KPFA Folio

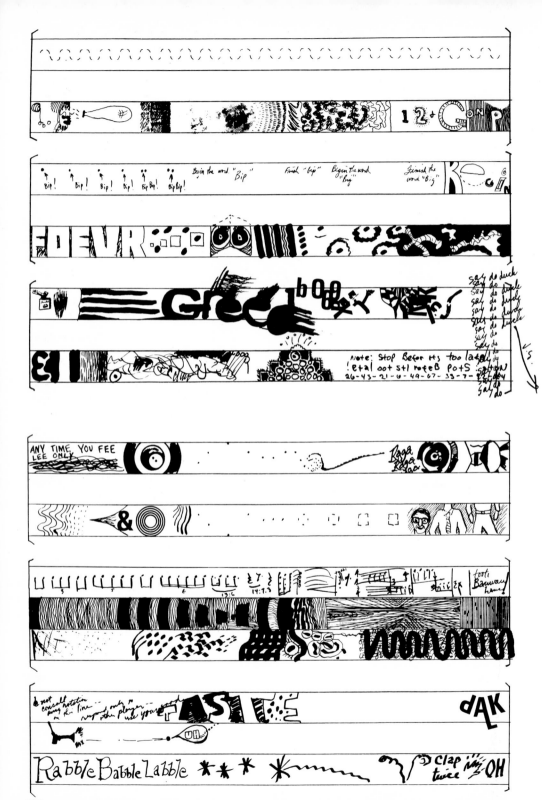

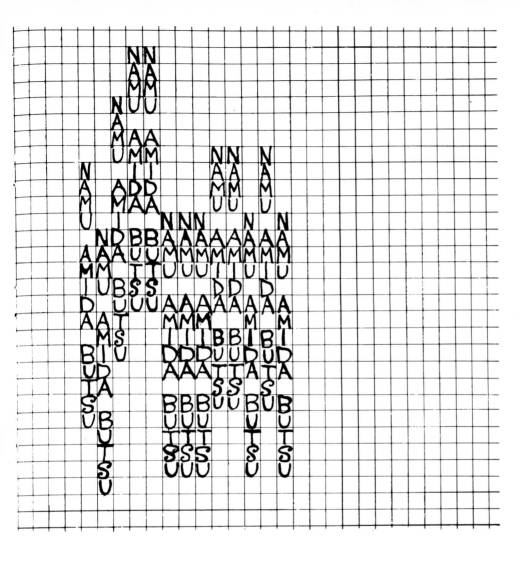

It is the performers almost more than the composer now who make the music—an approach, incidentally, dating at least back to the beginning of jazz. Although the controls that Bach used in his day were completely valid, we today have new ways of a multiplicity of input as our guides in composition. The inevitable question that arises is: Which is better, that the composer control what we do or that we ourselves play a major role in determining our own music? Each artist must determine this answer for himself, depending a great deal, of course, on what his motivations are. There is no universally acceptable answer. Both composer and performer have to make this decision. But it goes beyond that. This is not only a question of the artist's own intention, of his own way of working, of his own desire to set limits on results. More important in many ways is the acceptance by the audience of the demand put upon it for its own involvement—the degree to which it is, or is not, willing to become involved in the processes of creation. It is the audience itself which is being asked to become a group of participants. Its members, too, are beginning to be involved in the act, the process, of making art. They need to be willing to do so with an understanding of the reasons, and submit themselves to the necessary discipline.

The new open attitude toward composition in which the participation of the audience is an essential ingredient of the score is not limited to music but can also be seen in concrete poetry. Here is a "poem" by Jackson MacLow in which the directions read: "The reader begins at any square (empty squares are silences). He moves to any adjacent square horizontally, vertically, or diagonally, and continues this process until the end of the piece. Letters are read as any sound they can stand for in any language. When letters are repeated in a number of adjacent squares their sound may be continued for the duration thought of as equivalent to that number of squares, or they may be reiterated the same number of times as of squares. Letters can be read occasionally as one-letter words denoting the letters (e.g., "D" as "dee"). Groups of adjacent letters can be read as syllables, words, word-groups, and complete sentences. The following six possibilities should be produced by each performer during the piece: silences, phones, syllables, words, word-groups, and sentences (e.g., Namu Amida Butsu)." The relation to other scores in the book should be noted (*Parades and Changes*, Amirkhanian, Safdie architectural score).

The musical analogy is simple. The implication of open (as against closed) scoring in other fields gets more complex (because more demanding). Advocacy planning—the pluralistic involvement of members of communities in scoring the environment where they live and its future—is an important analogous situation. In previous times planners in their wisdom prepared plans *for* the people. Perhaps some may have been excellent plans, but there was a very basic issue missing. Today, in ghettos (and out) the residents themselves wish to engage actively in the scoring. They wish to participate in the action themselves, they wish to establish their own motivations under Resources (R) in the cycle and then go on to score the process. They no longer wish to be *scored for.* Advocacy planning uses questionnaires as a Resource (R) container from which community goals can be inventoried. Using these Resources, architects with their special technical abilities can write a score expressive of and including all of the community needs and desires.

Architecture has had its own failing in these "closed" systems of scoring. At Versailles this is apparent; but such latter-day Versailles as Le Corbusier's new city of Chandigarh, in India, the capital of Brazil called Brasilia, by Costa and Niemeyer, the British new towns or even Corbu's Unité d'Habitation in Marseilles, though often beautiful in visual form, lack congruence with the lifestyles of their people because the score was closed to them.

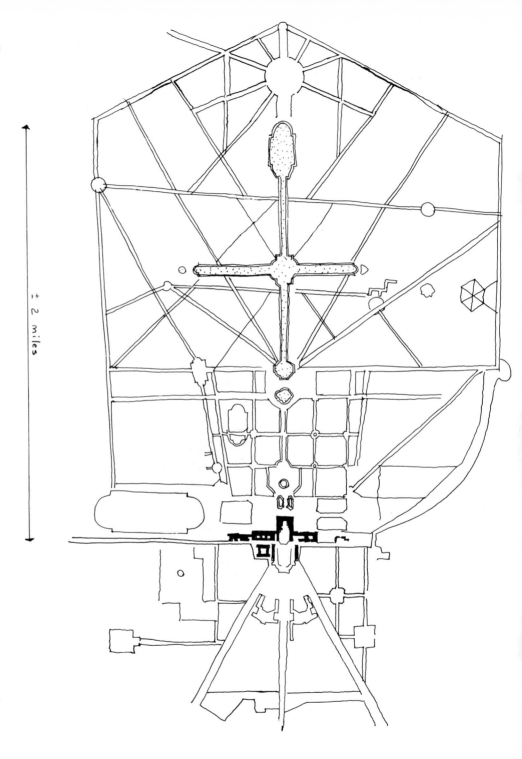

± 2 miles

A general tendency in the immediate past implied passivity on the part of the people as an audience for art; they have been receptacles for works developed by others—the artists. A form of specialization emerged—specialization in all the fields. Over the centuries artists have become specialists *for* the people. They expressed the highest and deepest felt essences of a culture; they painted *for* the people, they made music *for* the people, they built buildings *for* the people, they made (in politics) laws *for* the people. This created a dichotomy whose results are all around us. A dichotomy between the act of art and the act of life; between decision-making and results; between control and communication; between the score-maker and the scored-for; between the technician and the layman. It is a dichotomy which did not exist in primitive cultures where all the people were artists, nor does it even now exist among children or the free young people of the revolution who do not differentiate between the act of symbolization and the life process itself.

We are searching for ways to break down this dichotomy—for ways to allow people to enter into the act of making art as part of the art process—of open-ended scoring devices which will act as guides not dictators. These kinds of scores have the built-in possibilities for interaction between what is perceived beforehand and what emerges during the act. They allow the activity itself to generate its own results in process. They communicate but do not control. They energize and guide, they encourage, they evoke responses, they do not impose.

This redefines the role of the artist. It is no longer adequate for him to be a solitary "hero." He is repositioning himself in society and relating once again to the whole community. He is required to know more than the techniques of his special craft, and is becoming aware of art as a creative community experience by evolving scores which allow for creativity of others as well as himself. Thus he becomes part of a total configuration of all the people involved, including every age level and every ethnic group in our society.

This new attitude of the artist-as-scorer redefines the role even further. The artist now sees his work to be not only as a form maker himself but also as responsible for the creative drives of his total community. And as the artist is in a constant struggle with himself, more even than with outside influences, the score allows him to make this struggle explicit—that is, scoring not only makes his struggle and his choices visible to the community but, equally importantly, to the artist himself. Thus, the artist is in a constant search to define himself and his relation to his art and to relate these to his community. Both artist and his community can each play out their roles in full view of each other.

In the diagram of the RSVP cycles the artist-scorer's role is to make his own struggles explicit through the inner cycle. It is only as a resultant of his understanding of his own inner cycle that he can score the larger community cycle for his group. In this way the artist takes responsibility for his actions. By being explicit and by making his struggles and scores visible he accepts responsibility.

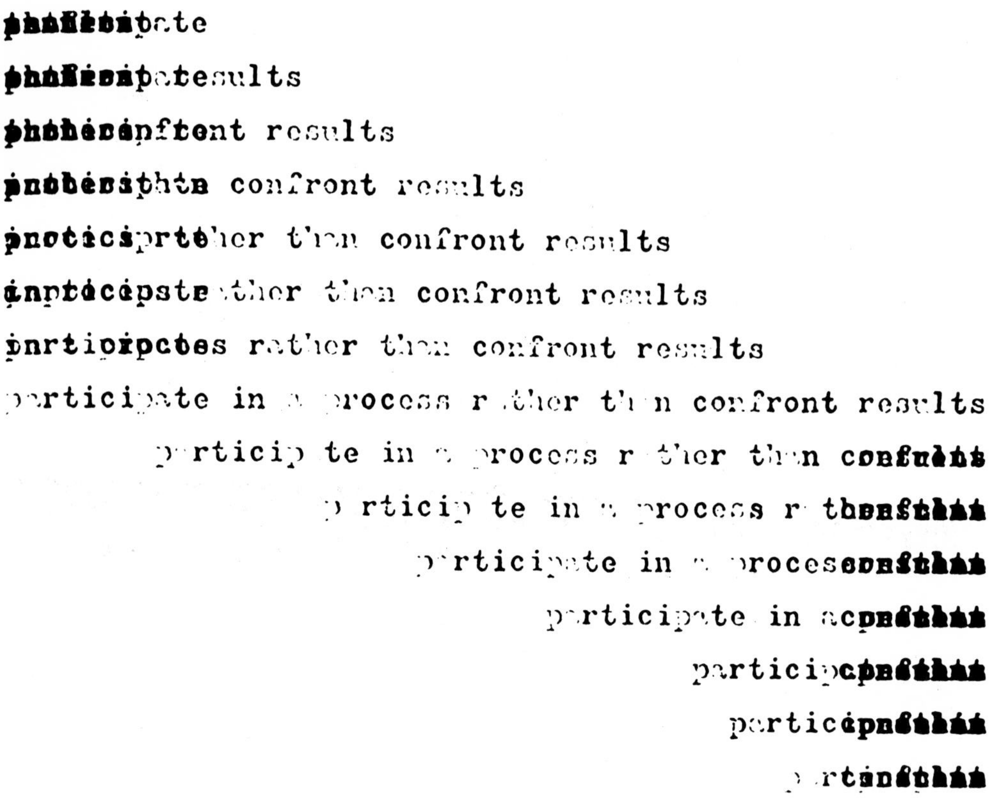

participate

participate results

participant results

confront results

participather than confront results

rather than confront results

rather than confront results

participate in a process rather than confront results

participate in a process rather than confront

participate in a process rather than

participate in a process rather than

participate in a

participate

participate

rather

Translation of "concrete poem" by Claus Bremer (1964).

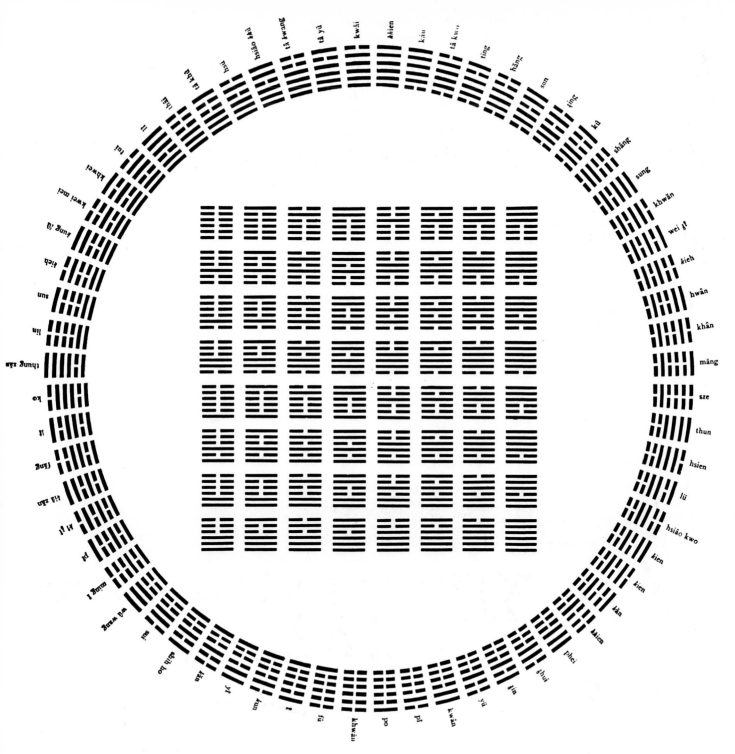

The Hexagrams, exhibited circularly and in a square, according to the natural process of development from the whole and divided lines, and the order of arrangement ascribed to Fu-hsi.

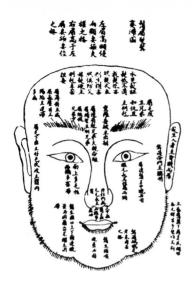

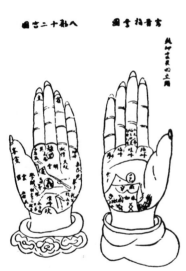

One of the very earliest scores that we know of is the *I Ching,* the book of change, developed in China at least three thousand years ago. For centuries the *I Ching* has served as a principle guide in China on how to govern a country, organize an enterprise, deal with people, conduct oneself under difficult conditions, and contemplate the future. It has been studied carefully by philosophers like Confucius and contemporary political leaders like Mao Tse-tung.

The comments of Jung on the *I Ching* stress the question of whether the universe is seen as determined or indeterminate; whether the man who plans for the future is any better off than the man who simply responds to what comes to him by chance. He implies, if the hexagrams fit use them, if not discard them.

The psychologist Dr. Paul Baum commented to me about his own experience with patients, "When a patient gets better he begins to have what he will often call 'good luck.' What this, in fact, turns out to mean is that favorable potentialities occur to him which he now finds himself capitalizing on. When we are in a neurotic state we engage ourselves in our bad luck and when we become 'healthy' we capitalize on our good luck, recognizing the

potential in chance events, and get involved with them. We then identify less with our bad luck. I think the *I Ching* was essentially an attempt to recognize that the road to success does not come from compulsivity, but it can result from a particularly creative way of using spontaneity, impulsivity, and randomness."

The *I Ching* starts from a series of lines which are either unbroken _____ or broken __ __ . The unbroken lines represent Yang and the broken Yin—masculine and feminine, sun and shade, hardness and softness. From these two types of lines, trigrams were developed which refer both to natural phenomena such as sky, water, earth, and so forth, and also to human behavior. Thus, the relationship between humans in nature is clearly established symbolically. It has profound ecological as well as psychological implications.

The trigrams are combined to form sixty-four hexagrams which categorize the working man's sixty-four human conditions. Each hexagram is divided into six typical events of evolving behavior.

A person interested in his future would follow standard ceremonial procedure such as tossing coins or sorting yarrow stalks to select his hexagram. When he

Chinese physiognomy chart based on characteristics of hair growth for prognosticating one's aptitude and fortune. (For instance, knitted brow indicates violent sibling rivalry.)

Palmistry chart for reading of wealth and prosperity.

Parallel diagrams showing the process of action and interaction of Yin-Yang and the universe.

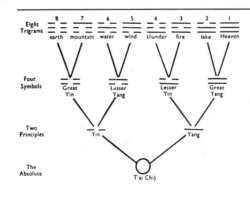

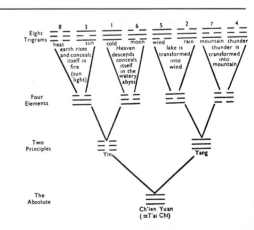

found his hexagram he looked up the oracular message which gave him an insight into his future fortunes and recommended the courses of action for him to take under the circumstances.

A line of a hexagram, representing a given event in one's life, may be compared to a note in a melody. The note itself possesses at least two potentialities. As an isolated note it exhibits a fixed frequency of a certain number of vibrations per second with a characteristic pitch. But when it is finally expressed in music, an equally important characteristic comes to the fore. It loses its individualism in the orchestral offering. Its pervasiveness becomes significant. The final effect of the note is then determined by its association with other notes and no-notes, with its rendition by particular instruments, with its position relative to the beat rhythm, and many other factors. This is the inherent vitality of music. The hexagrams of the I Ching *may be looked upon as a comprehensive series of psychic scores covering the spectrum of human responses.*

R. G. H. Siu,
The Man of Many Qualities

The *I Ching* as a score was a way for each person to plug into the ineffable rhythms of the universe. The Chinese did not consider the *I Ching* either magical or mystical—simply a scoring system which described a person's interrelatedness with everything else which was happening in the universe and about to happen—man and man, man and nature.

Tarot cards, like the *I Ching*, are an ancient system of divination; mystical scores for describing the future through preordained symbols. The cards create a kind of universal pictorial language in which each relates to past and future events. When the cards are thrown in a systematic way they enable both singly and in combination a glimpse into the future.

WHEEL of FORTUNE.

The Tarot pack of cards consists of seventy-eight cards—fifty-eight contained in four suits called the Minor Arcana and twenty-two known as the Major Arcana. The Major Arcana are, it is thought, a concentrated version of Hermetic philosophy as interpreted in the Kabala, in alchemy, magic, and astrology.

These picture-symbols are drawn from a deep store of images common to all men, everywhere, in all ages; images drawn from what has been called "the collective unconscious." They appear in our dreams, in the creative fantasies of poets, in the visions of saints and prophets. We see before we say; words are labels for man's visual imagination; thinking in pictures is a basic activity of the human mind.

Eden Gray, *The Tarot Revealed*

"Unlike despotic orthodoxies a symbol favors independence. Only a symbol can deliver a man from the slavery of words and formulae and allow him to attain to the possibility of thinking freely. It is impossible to avoid the use of symbols if one desires to penetrate into the secrets" (Oswald Wirth).

Papus, *The Tarot of the Bohemians*

The Minor Arcana consists of fifty-six cards equally divided into four suits comparable to the suits of our present-day playing cards:

Wands = clubs	strife and	
Cups = hearts	misfortune	
Swords = spades	money and	
Pentacles = diamonds	interest	
Associated with	*Identified with*	
enterprise and	fire	
glory	water	
love and	air	
happiness	earth	

DIAGRAM   THE ANCIENT CELTIC METHOD

Significator is placed in center.

No. 1   This covers him.
No. 2   This crosses him.
No. 3   This is beneath him.
No. 4   This is behind him.
No. 5   This crowns him.
No. 6   This is before him.
No. 7   What he fears.
No. 8   Family opinion.
No. 9   His hopes.
No. 10   Final outcome.

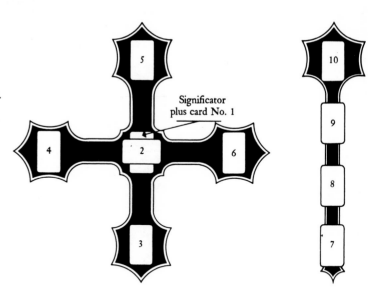

Significator plus card No. 1

DIAGRAM   THE TREE OF LIFE METHOD

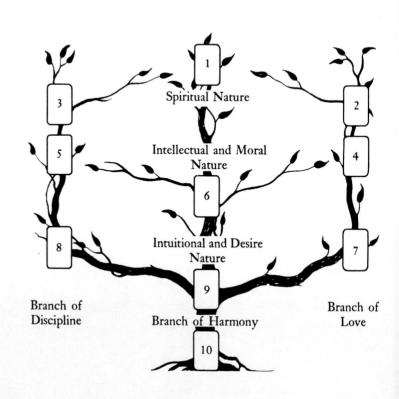

Spiritual Nature

Intellectual and Moral Nature

Intuitional and Desire Nature

Branch of Discipline

Branch of Harmony

Branch of Love

Daath Pack

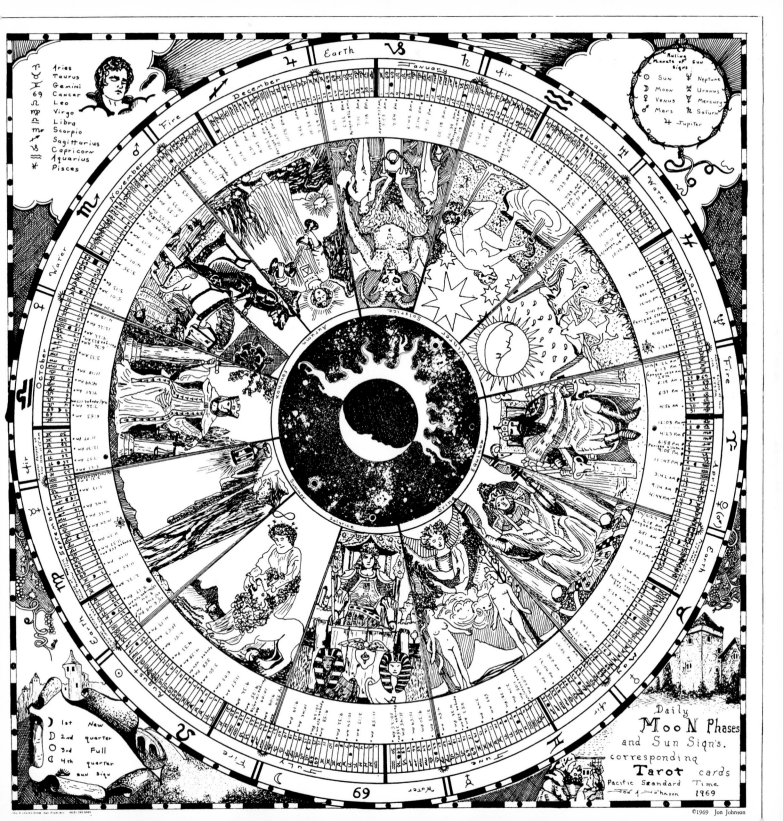

Daily
MooN Phases
and Sun Signs.
corresponding
Tarot cards
Pacific Standard Time
1969

©1969 Jon Johnson

As with the *I Ching*, it is important to note the relationship between the human condition and its counterpart in nature.

The cards are thrown in certain preordained ways and both by their own interior meanings, their adjacency to the other cards, and the totality of all the cards together forecast what the future will bring.

There are several methods for arranging the cards in a score: the ancient Celtic method and the tree of life method are favorites.

The relationship of the Tarot cards to the *I Ching* hexagrams is remarkable; both deal with universal ideas and problems facing us all in life situations. Both connect us with the subconscious activities of the human mind and with natural processes. Both deal with archetypal examples of what Jung has called the "collective unconscious." In both the divination process itself requires a letting go of the intellect—an acknowledgment of the rhythmic and unconscious forces at work in the universe. If we can give way to these forces and think of ourselves as part of the universal processes of living, of time in space, then we can release ourselves from preconceptions and hangups which prevent and block creativity. One of the important functions of scores is to make possible and accepted nonrational means of "getting at" problems. Both the Tarot cards and the *I Ching* have been used by musicians such as Pauline Olivieros and Morton Subotnik as compositional devices. Pauline Olivieros has said "I mix chance and choice somewhat scandalously" (*Notations,* John Cage).

Astrological charts, too, are examples of mystical scores. The Zodiac is a great imagined circle extending around the heavens, so as to take in the different orbits of the planets as well as the earth's satellite, the moon, in the middle of which is the ecliptic or path of the sun. Within this great circle are the twelve signs of the Zodiac (man's score of the planets and their influences). Each sign has its own personality, spiritualism, strength, and weakness. The influences of each sign are carried into each person, depending on which month (sign) or planet he is born under.

There is emerging evidence that the influence of the heavenly bodies once thought to be completely illogical *is* more than mystical or poetic. Many of the biological timing devices which control the behavioral activities of animals, formerly thought to be purely instinctual, are more and more found to be related to the influence of the sun and moon. Perhaps indeed, these astrological "scores" will be shown to have not only intuitively divined validity but biological validity as well.

These scores then become guides to all the other processes going on at the same time—at all levels of existence. They are ways for us to relate to events and processes normally hidden from us by our usual mechanisms of cause and effect or the value systems imposed on us by Western culture.

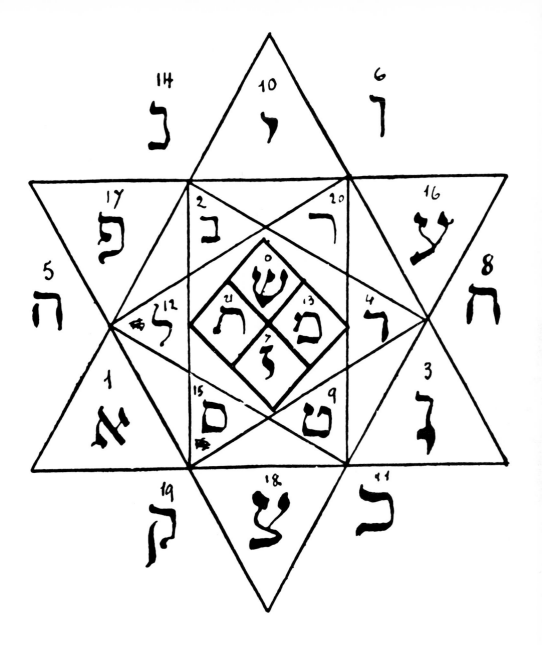

The Astronomical Tarot. Signs of the Zodiac and circumpolar constellation affinities with the Tarot (Pentacle of Oswald Wirth).

In addition to the *I Ching* and the Tarot there are other comparable scoring techniques which deal with the effects of universal spiritual forces on human behavior. Navajo sand paintings are scores for lengthy dances and sings in which prototypical invocations and folkways are performed to heal and cure what are primarily psychologically derived disorders.

The inevitable relation between these sings and modern theatre is striking, as are the close and organic correlations between graphics, poetry, music, dance, and the environment. Like many other scores for primitive rituals, the Navajo sand paintings relate all the arts together into an environmental event with profound personal consequences.

Sandpainting is an integral part of the Navajo healing ritual which also includes songs and prayers. The sandpainting depicts the chief etiological factors held responsible for the patient's condition; and the curing chant is made up of procedures that exorcise evil and invoke the supernatural spirits who are able to correct the harm.

The Endless Snake sandpainting commemorates the flight of a young girl in the Navajo Beautyway myth. It depicts her encounter with five endless snake guards in a cave where she spent the night. The encircling guardian is the black snake with spots. Water jug and white cloud are paired eastern guards at the entrance. The figure is open toward the east in the Navajo fashion for all dwellings.

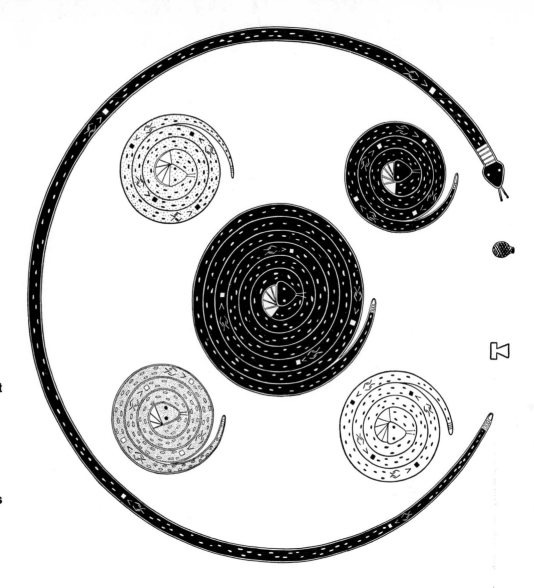

CHARITY

BUYING PILES OF OLD CLOTHES

WASHING THEM
IN ALL-NIGHT LAUNDROMATS

GIVING THEM BACK
TO USED-CLOTHES STORES

(MARCH 7)

POSE

CARRYING CHAIRS THROUGH THE CITY

SITTING DOWN HERE AND THERE

PHOTOGRAPHED

PIX LEFT ON SPOT

GOING ON

(MARCH 21)

SIX ORDINARY HAPPENINGS
BY ALLAN KAPROW

ORDINARY PHOTOS BY CAROL BOWEN

FINE!

PARKING CARS IN RESTRICTED ZONES

WAITING NEARBY FOR COP

SNAPSHOT OF GETTING TICKET

DETAILED REPORT

SENDING PIX, REPORTS, FINES TO COPS

(APRIL 4)

SHAPE

SHOES, BODIES
ON STREETS, SIDEWALKS, FIELDS

SPRAY PAINTING THEIR SILHOUETTES

REPORTS AND PHOTOS IN NEWSPAPER

(APRIL 16)

GIVEAWAY

STACKS OF DISHES
LEFT ON STREET CORNERS

PHOTOGRAPHED

NEXT DAY, PHOTOGRAPHED

(MAY 7)

PURPOSE
(Variations on a theme of Tomas Schmit)

MAKING A MOUNTAIN OF SAND

MOVING IT REPEATEDLY
UNTIL THERE IS NO MOUNTAIN

RECORDING THE WORK SOUNDS

RERECORDING THEM
UNTIL THERE IS NO SOUND OF WORK

LISTENING TO THE TAPES

(MAY 23)

A series of events presented by OTHER WAYS. Those interested in participating in any or all, should attend preliminary meetings on the dates indicated, 8:30 p.m., at East Campus, Dwight Way (Haste Bldg., Rm. 101). The Happenings will occur on the next day(s).

The simplest new form of scoring for interaction between the environment, people, and other elements is the environmental event or "happening," where a score is devised which establishes certain preconditions and then allows for freedom in process. The happening as an environmental art form is based on the scoring idea that the process is an essential ingredient in the making of environments. The process is usually loosely delineated and consists of activities, not how they are carried out.

In its earliest forms the happening has inevitable connections to abstract expressionist painting, in which the action formed the painting but then went out into the environment to include the outside world and objective (as well as subjective) elements. In the happening, simple directions are given, a place is chosen for the event, and (sometimes) props are used. What transpires, however, is largely the result of the participants' own input and interaction, since the event is, in most instances, not overly structured. This is not to imply, however, that no structure exists. It does. The organizer of the happening has lined out certain parameters, he has established an environment, he has (by choosing location, time, and very often by establishing attitudes) guided the resultant form into an organized work. The designer of a happening catalyzes actions in certain directions, but does not determine what precisely emerges. Happenings are not chaos—they may appear chaotic, but when carefully thought out and programmed they can result in superb works: scored but not completely controlled. The event becomes a kind of instant symbiosis between the participants and their environment.

Ann Halprin has extended the happening into two important and mutually supportive directions. One emphasizes the ritualistic basis of art and life and establishes basic—even primitive—human responses as the major structuring elements for her events. On *Myths* (with graphic scores by Patric Hickey) she comments:

Myths *are experimental. The performers, members of the Dancers' Workshop Company, are unrehearsed. What unfolds is a spontaneous exploration of theatre ideas.* Myths *are meant to evoke our long-buried and half-forgotten selves. Each evening will explore a different relationship between the audience and performers, and through our awareness and interactions the audience will evolve collective images. The audience should not be bound by accustomed passivity, by static self images.*

Myths *are your myths. They are an experiment in mutual creation.*

The "audiences" were, by and large, neither homogeneous nor an in-group. They were a mixture of hippies, students, all types of businessmen, dancers, architects, city planners, psychotherapists, tourists, families and their children. In short, a cross section of an urban society.

Although each Myth was different, the central idea of every evening was to release people's buried creativity by answering one of their basic needs through ritual.

The experience, of course, was not like that of a frightened nightclub patron pressured by a performer or friend to get up on stage and make a fool of himself. Certain general conditions were suggested to the group in the briefing room. Thereafter, anyone was free to participate or observe. A few people left. But the vast majority stayed, participated, even participated ecstatically. For some it was simply fun, for some a bore, for some extraordinarily sensual, for some a happening, for some a kind of atavistic tribal reawakening. For me, it was all these things—and a new exploration of communal art.

People sought individual freedom, found it, and found community as well. Order through freedom: freed from the constraints of a normal "performance," the whole group found

its own social and artistic structures. At times the birth of this new and more natural order seemed chaotic—the public would alter the instructions, the sound, or the physical environment, and there were periods of great destruction and reformation. During these phases a few people became disturbed and left the building. However, most of these who were not in the midst of the action just withdrew to some quiet spot on the side, and eventually rejoined the group after a new period of order had been established—an order completely real in that it reflected deeply rooted intuitive drives emerging from a collectively subconscious energy, resulting in archetypal experiences.

One aspect of the original idea was to explore different relationships between audience and performer. I, and the audiences, assumed that total audience involvement would be either chaotic or impossible. During the first few Myths, *the company members were used as a core group: catalysts, demonstrators, guides. But soon the audience transcended this, the company members began to merge with them, and by the third* Myth *we were mutually creating events.*

I am interested in a theatre where everything is experienced for the first time, and I have stripped away all ties with conventional dance forms: in the lives of individual performers, their training, rehearsals, and performances form a process which in itself is an experience. I have come back to the ritualistic beginnings of art as a sharpened expression of life, extending every kind of perception. I want to participate in events of supreme authenticity, to involve people with their environment so that life is lived whole.

Perhaps my role is being redefined. I am coming to see the artist in another light. He is no longer a solitary hero figure, but rather a synthesizer who brings together differences and works to evoke the art within us all. This is the true meaning of a seminal theatre.

Ann Halprin, *Creation*

TH TWO— ATONEMENT   D/W SF

21 DIVISADERO STREET   ANN HALPRIN, DIRECTOR

AN FRANCISCO, CALIF.   PATRIC HICKEY,

ALL 1967   ENVIRONMENTALIST

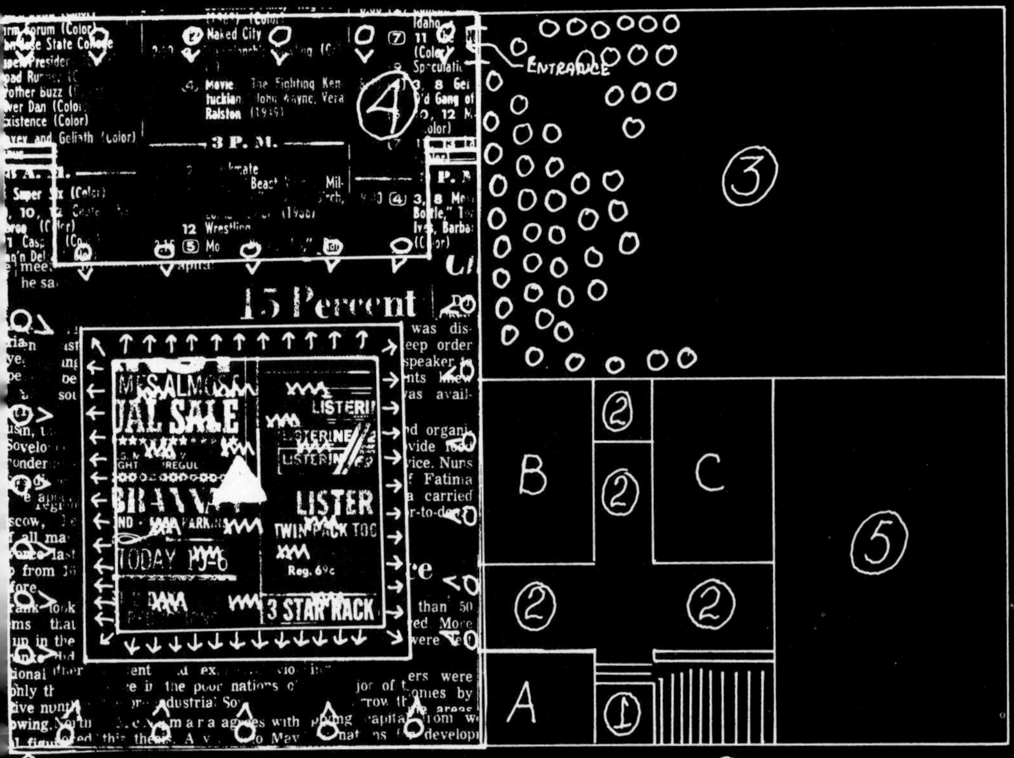

SCALE: 1" = 8'

CODE:

→   Audience standing facing in direction arrow indicates.

⊃> Spotlight, 150 wt. white focused direction indicated at 6 feet elevation

XXX Columns of newspaper 12 feet elevation

▲   Percussionist

Ω   Position for aud. briefing.

①- Stairwell to street
②- Corridor
③- Small studio
④- Large studio
⑤- Lounge
A- Rest room
B- Office
C- Storage

NOTE:

Entire room (walls and floor) covered in newspaper from one day's edition. Only one selected page used, in complete repetition.

MYTH FOUR – TOTEM
321 DIVISADERO STREET
SAN FRANCISCO, CALIF.
FALL 1967

D/W S F
ANN HALPRIN, DIRECTOR
PATRIC HICKEY,
ENVIRONMENTALIST

MYTH NINE – STORY
321 DIVISADERO STREET
SAN FRANCISCO, CALIF.
WINTER 1967

D/W S F
ANN HALPRIN, DIRECTOR
PATRIC HICKEY,
ENVIRONMENTALIST

SCALE: 1"=8'
CODE:

□→ Chair, arrow indicat-
ing position audience
member is facing

⊝ Suspended, 60 wt
lamp; elevation
varies from 1 foot
to 8 feet from floor.

▲ Percussionist

① - Stairwell to street
② - Corridor
③ - Small studio
④ - Large studio
⑤ - Lounge
A - Rest room
B - Office
C - Storage

NOTE:
During experience, bulbs
are replaced one by
one, using one selection
of color. When completed
a short pause, then action
repeated with new color.
Ranges from colored lamps
to clear white.

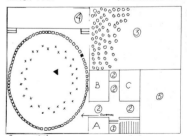

SCALE: 1"=8'
CODE:

□ Audience seated
in folding chairs.

× Candles

▲ Percussionist

⊠ Candle attendant

○ Position for audience
briefing

① - Stairwell from street
② - Corridor
③ - Small studio
④ - Large studio
⑤ - Lounge
A - Rest room
B - Office
C - Storage

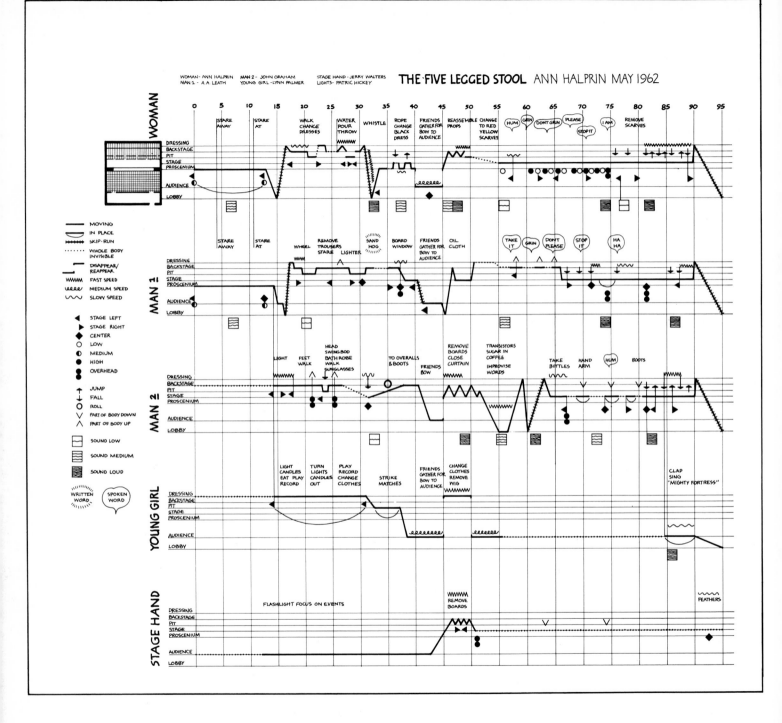

THE·FIVE LEGGED STOOL ANN HALPRIN MAY 1962

WOMAN - ANN HALPRIN   MAN 2 - JOHN GRAHAM   STAGE HAND - JERRY WALTERS
MAN 1 - A.A. LEATH   YOUNG GIRL - LYNN PALMER   LIGHTS - PATRIC HICKEY

This same system of scoring and choreographing when used as a creative device for professional dancers has established a selection (V) process for more formalized choreography. It serves in its own way as a kind of latticelike structuring mechanism often used in computer analysis whereby multivariable interaction and permutations can be developed which are literally impossible through the preconceptions of a single mind. The choreographer establishes an environment and a generalized "line of action," but does not form the dance in the usual way of telling the group what the patterns should be. Instead, she invents situations which evoke specific kinds of interactions. As the dance proceeds over long and arduous workshop sessions, selectivity (S) both by the choreographer and the group itself is exercised and finally a dance emerges, based on the original score which has been altered by a series of Valuactions (V) which are then "scored into" a theatre piece. In this way *5-Legged Stool* and *Parades and Changes* were scored (see scores figure below). It is safe to say that these theatre pieces could never have been choreographed through the usual techniques—and the scoring technique influenced the results profoundly.

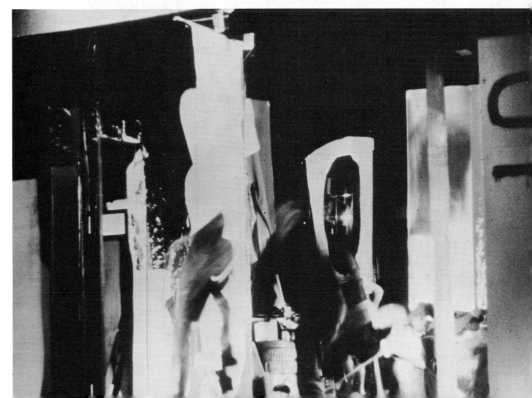

On the development of the score for *Parades and Changes* Ann Halprin comments:

I was concerned about finding a way for the collaborating artists to work and exchange ideas together and mutually develop a Performance (P) and also for dancers to be free to respond most fully with their individual capacities as an input into the score. Morton Subotnik, the composer, originated a method called cell-blocks, i.e.,

CELL-BLOCKS

Musician

1	2	3	4
5	6	7	8
9	10	11	12

Choreography

1	2	3	4
5	6	7	8
9	10	11	12

Sculpture

1	2	3
4	5	6

the cell-block method meant that each collaborating artist, musician, dancer-choreographer, lighting designer, sculptor, coordinator, evolved a series of sound actions, movement actions, light action, environmental or sculptural actions in discrete thematic ideas called cell-blocks. For example, in Morton Subotnik's score of cell-blocks: 1. might represent "live-music" on a horn—single sustained sound; 2. electronic sound; 3. percussion rhythmic pattern; 4. Bach's Brandenburg Concerto. These cell-blocks went on to a variety of ten different sound events. The choreography included: 1. dress and undress; 2. stomp dance; 3. embrace; 4. costume parade; 5. move with scaffold; 6. paper dance, etc.

Patric Hickey and Charles Ross developed their own light and sculpture events in the same way. All cell-blocks were mutually developed so that they were, in fact, interchangeable. The basis of selecting events was that all of them could be interchangeable at any time and still be extremely diverse. This offered the opportunity of being able to go to any theatre and immediately adapt to the peculiar needs of that theatre by selecting out of our cell-blocks what we felt would work best in that particular physical space, and with that particular audience. The independency of these cell-blocks also plugs into internal needs within the company personnel. As new members come in, others leave, each artist can function according to his unique attributes, that is, in Europe, Folke Rabe, composer, used his own cell-blocks while in New York, Morton used still another set, his own.

When we performed Parades and Changes *in Stockholm, we used the score principle to present three evenings of* Parades and Changes *at the Stadesterean Theatre, and, by simply changing the selection of cell-blocks and the order, both this way → and that way ↓, we could derive a totally different result.*

We also discovered that by changing the order both → and ↓ we were required to create new ways of dealing with transitions, which in itself challenged all of us into creating fresh material for each program.

Parades and Changes *has been performed on a street mall in Fresno, at an opera house in Warsaw, in Stockholm, at Hunter College in New York City, in numerous campus theatres, and never has the score had the same resultant performance. The cell-blocks principle is so organized that not only are all the parts independent and therefore can be reassembled, assembled, and reassembled in infinite combinations, each combination generating a different quality, but the sequence can start from any point. For example, what might start the performance one night, could another night be the end. In terms of development new cell-blocks can be added, others omitted so that over a period of several years the same score can be in operation but entirely new cell-blocks (materials) can be inserted to the extent that the original Parades and Changes has very little resemblance to the new one. I point this out because we ordinarily think of time in regard to the length of time of the performance. Here I'm suggesting that we think of time over a period of years as well.*

This related it to ecological scoring.

MASTER SCORE PARTS

Version I

Artists	Time 5 min.	10	15	20 25
Musician	1	2	5	8
Lighting	2	3	6	9
Dancers/ Chorus	3	3	7	9
Environmentalist	3	4	7	3

Version II

	Time 5 min.	10	15	20
Music	3	10	1	X
Light	4	11	4	X
Dance	7	12	no dance X	X
Environment	8	1	5	6

Version III

Music	3	8	1	8
Light	1	9	2	9
Dance	5	11	4	9
Environment	6	2	6	10

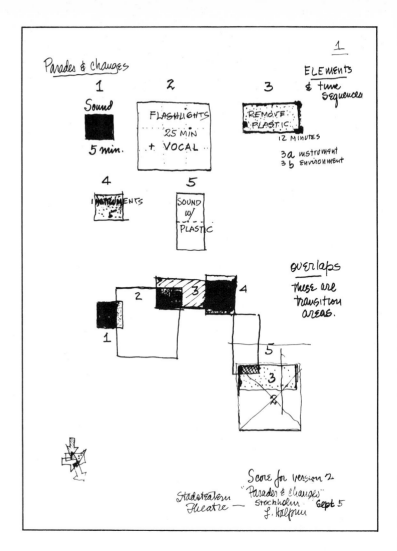

Parts of the master score for
Parades and Changes, **developed in**
San Francisco.

38

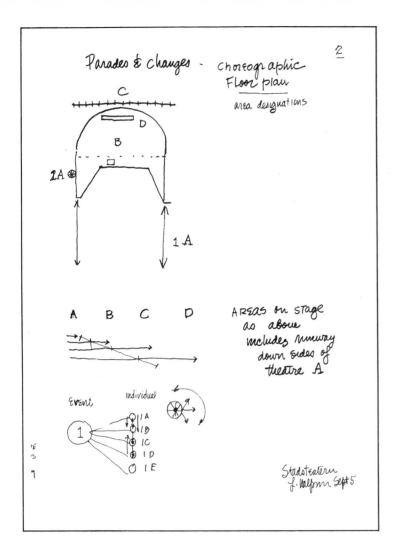

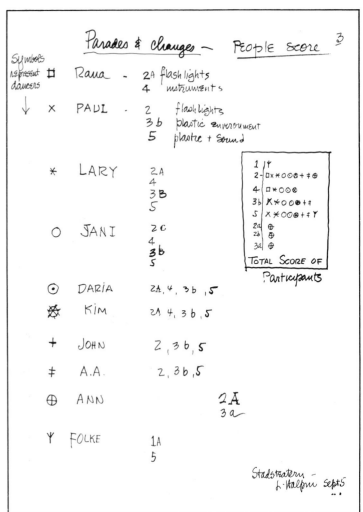

One version of *Parades and Changes* as performed in Stockholm, Statsteatern Theater, September, 1966. It was assembled in the theatre the day before the performance according to the physical environment, and using the modules (Version III of master score), and was organized into the dance and graphically scored by the author. "Elements" refer to modular sections of the dance—the score indicates how these were to be put together; overlaps (transitions), the people involved, their participation, and the position of activities in the theatre.

The Parts of the Limbs

STUDY IN BALLET STYLE
(Use of Parts of the Leg)

Suggested music: The Coda of Act II
from the "Swan Lake" ballet.

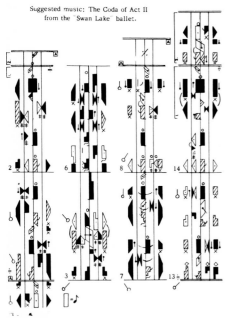

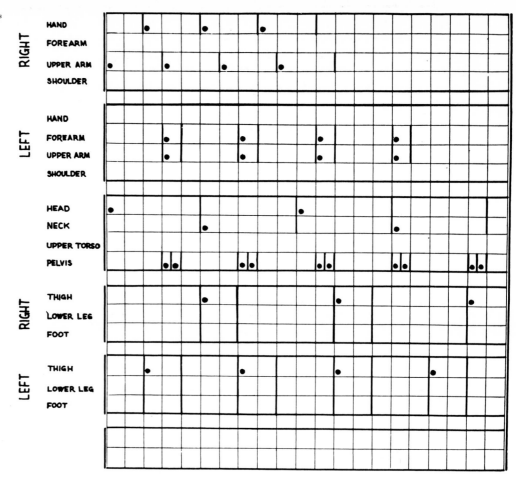

These former theatre scores are quite different in intent and purpose from the scoring techniques of Labanotation and Eshkol. These two scoring systems are dance notations which enable choreographers to transmit the dance movement they have preconceived to another dancer or choreographer. These scores control the future since they deal with an accepted and known set of gestures and movements which they describe with precision.

The purpose is not compositional but controlling, just as Bach's musical score was controlling. These two dance notation systems are quite different in their technique but similar in purpose. Both are extremely useful in transmitting information over space and time about gesture and movement through graphic scores.

Labanotation was developed in Europe by the dancer, Rudolf Laban and is the most widely taught and used of the dance notation systems. This particular section is a study in the use of limbs.

Two scores from the Eshkol system are built up of time and position symbols. The complete system is explained in *Movement Notation,* by Noa Eshkol and Abraham Wachman.

1 = 15°

	1	2	3	4	5	6	7	8	9	10	11	12	13
LEFT ARM o								(0/0)					
o						(18/0)	(12/0)	(6/0)(6/6)	(6/12)(6/6)				
o	(21/6)	(13/6)	(13/6)(12)	(6/0)(6/6)	(12/0)	(18/6)	(18/6)	(6/6)	(6/21)(6/6)	(9/0)(6/6)	(3/3)	(3/3)	
o													
RIGHT ARM o								(12/0)					(6/9)(3/6)	(18/3)(9)
o						(18/6)	(0/0)	(6/6)(6/6)	(12/0)(6)			(12/9)(3/6)	(12/3)(9)
o	(3/6)	(6/6)	(6/6)(12)	(12/0)	(12/0)	(6/6)	(6/6)	(0/0)	(6/0)(6/6)	(3/0)(6/6)	(18/9)	(6/3)
o													
RIGHT LEG o	(0/0)(6/6)	(13/6)(6/6)	(13/6)	(1/0)(6/6)	(1/0)	(15/0)(6/6)	(6/0)	(3/0)	(15/6)(6/6)	(3/0)	(10/6)*	(6/3)(6/6)
o					(12/0)(6/6)			(0/0)(6/6)	(0/0)		(18/6)
□	□(6/6)	□(6)	□	□(6/6)	□	□(6/6)			□(6/6)	□	
LEFT LEG o	(0/0)(6/6)	(11/6)(6/6)	(11/6)	(23/0)(6/6)	(23/0)	(9/0)(6/6)	(0/0)	(15/0)	(9/0)(6/6)	(0/0)	(14/6)	(15/0)
o					(12/0)(6/6)			(9/0)				(9/0)
□	□(6/6)	□(6/6)	□	□(6/6)	□	□(6/6)	□	□	□(6/6)	□	□	□

Ex. VII. Thirteen Positions of the Body. (Note the scale: 1 = 15°). The whole torso remains in Zero Position in all the positions, and is therefore not represented on the page, The first four positions are broadly described below.

(1) All the limbs are in Zero Position.
(2) The legs are in "first position", and the arms midway between the "first" and "second position" of Classical Ballet.
(3) The feet are a small pace apart, the legs turned out; the right arm extended to the right side, horizontal to the ground; the left arm raised almost to the left side of the head.
(4) Similar to the third, except that the feet and legs are parallel to one another and the arms rotated so that the palm of the right hand faces upward, and the palm of the left hand towards the right.

Note.—In position 12, the single asterisk indicates that the right leg crosses in front of the left.

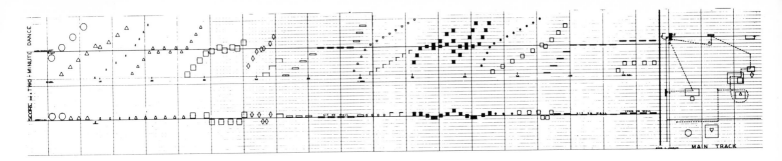

Dance notation by Lawrence Halprin for a two minute event—early use of motation to design for motion through space (not for gesture).

The scores for the theatre pieces and for *Myths* use plots of people in space and against time. Elements in the environment, too, are involved to a degree in the score; chairs are moved, platforms are used, and so forth. But precision of sequence and timing are not significant and the score covers at the most a period of several hours.

Increasingly, we face the need for organizing and controlling large numbers of people performing different activities in different places but with a common or interrelated motive. The scores for these kinds of activities are very similar to the theatre pieces or happenings which we have been observing. They deal with the same variables of people

or space over time and their interrelatedness. The major difference is the degree of precision and, of course, the purpose of the activities. Here are several very similar and related scores which control with a varying degree of precision and have different purposes.

The most controversial play of the football season, the game-winning play for Minnesota over Northwestern November 1, 1941, and declared to be illegal by Lynn Waldorf, Northwestern coach, who did not see it, is diagrammed on this page. It is reproduced partly from visual memory and partly from the replies to questions asked in the Minnesota dressing room after the game. Infallibility is not claimed, but the diagram is believed to be correct.

This observer, seated in the press box, must confess to being caught napping, as were eleven Northwestern players and 64,464 customers. He looked up from charting the preceding play at the exact moment that Gene Flick, the Minnesota center, scooped up the ball and threw it to Bud Higgins, who ran 41 yards for a touchdown that won the game, 8–7.

A picture of the alignment of the Minnesota players at the moment is clear and vivid still. The positions of the Northwestern men are guesswork, but approximately correct. What happened immediately after the play was set in motion is not vouched for as exact, since twenty-two men were moving rapidly, but it, too, is advanced as approximately correct.

Northwestern, with a touchdown, was leading Minnesota, 7–2, in the third period and

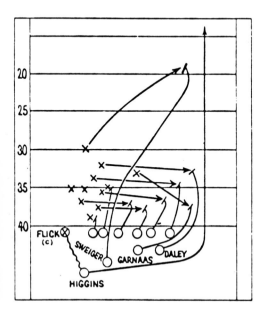

One of the most famous and controversial football plays. A score for action over time.

Route 519—Dallas to Waco, Tex. —109.0 m.

Pavement and gravel. A section of the King of Trails. Thru a prosperous level and rolling farm country.

Designated as U. S. Highway 81 from Alvarado.

Dallas City Map, Route 486.

Hiway No.	Mileage	
68	0.0	DALLAS, Commerce & Akard Sts. Southwest on Commerce St.
68	0.5	Houston St. beyond courthouse; left. Cross long viaduct 0.9.
68	1.8	Fork at end of viaduct; right on Zangs Boulevard, and avoid left 1.9.
68	2.5	Thru gate on double drive.
68	3.0	End of boulevard; right on Davis St.
68	4.2	Edgefield Ave.; left.
68	5.2	Jim Town Rd., at filling sta.; right.
68	5.9	End of road; left.
68	6.4	Right-hand road at trolley; right.
68	7.7	4-cor.; left.
68	14.0	DUNCANVILLE.
68	14.1	Fork; right.
68	19.6	CEDAR HILL, at bar stand. Bear right, then left.
68	26.5	End of road; right.
68	28.6	4-cor.; right 1 blk.; left.
68	28.7	MIDLOTHIAN, 4-cor. Right.
68	31.0	Left-hand road; left.
68	35.5	End of road; left.
68	37.7	Right-hand road; right.
68	38.1	VENUS.
68	45.7	4-cor.; right.
2	45.8	ALVARADO, 4-cor. at filling sta. Left.
2	56.3	GRANDVIEW, 4-cor. beyond RR. Right.
2	64.4	ITASCA, 4-cor. at banks. Right.
2	64.5	Left-hand road beyond RR; left.
2	69.6	LOVELACE.
2	75.0	End of road beyond RR underpass; right.
2	75.4	HILLSBORO, at courthouse. Keep ahead on Waco St.
2	75.9	Fork beyond underpass; right on Dexter St.
2	76.2	Abbott Ave.; left.
2	85.1	ABBOTT.
2	90.8	Right-hand road; right then left.
2	91.2	WEST.
2	100.5	ELM MOTT.
2	104.0	LACY.
		Left 108.1 is Route 572 (Highway 6) to Houston. Cross Brazos River 108.6 onto Washington Ave.
2	109.0	WACO, Washington Ave. & 5th St., at courthouse.
		Left on 5th St. is Route 520 (Highway 2) to San Antonio.

Car rallye score from Dallas to Waco, Texas.

For Astronauts Aboard Apollo 11, There Are 88 Steps to the Moon and Back

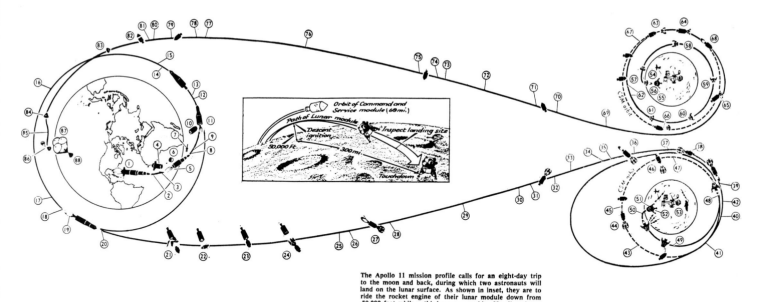

The Apollo 11 mission profile calls for an eight-day trip to the moon and back, during which two astronauts will land on the lunar surface. As shown in inset, they are to ride the rocket engine of their lunar module down from 50,000 feet while a third crewman orbits 69 miles above.

THE 88 STEPS

1. First stage of Saturn 5 ignites; liftoff.
2. First stage powered flight.
3. First stage cutoff.
4. First stage separates, drops away; second stage ullage.*
5. Second stage ignites.
6. Connection between first and second stages is jettisoned.
7. Launch escape tower is jettisoned.
8. Second stage powered flight.
9. Second stage cutoff.
10. Second stage separates, drops away; third stage ullage.
11. Third stage ignites.
12. Third stage powered flight.
13. Third stage cutoff.
14. Earth parking orbit.
15. Begin systems status checks.
16. Adjust guidance system of command and service module (CSM).
17. Orient for translunar injection.
18. Third stage ullage.
19. Third stage re-ignites.
20. Translunar injection.
21. CSM separates from rest of vehicle.
22. CSM turns around 180 degrees.
23. CSM docks with lunar module (LM), which is still attached to third stage.
24. CSM and LM separate from third stage.
25. Adjust CSM inertial guidance system.
26. Orient spacecraft for midcourse correction.
27. Ignite service propulsion engine.
28. First midcourse correction.
29. System status checks; eat and sleep periods; transmit data to earth.

30. Adjust CSM inertial guidance system.
31. Orient spacecraft for midcourse correction.
32. Midcourse correction, if required.
33. System status checks; eat and sleep period; transmit data to earth.
34. Adjust CSM inertial guidance system.
35. Orient spacecraft for midcourse correction.
36. Final midcourse correction, if necessary.
37. Adjust CSM inertial guidance system.
38. Orient spacecraft attitude for lunar orbit insertion.
39. Lunar orbit insertion.
40. Begin lunar orbit.
41. Adjust CSM inertial guidance system.
42. Circularize lunar orbit.
43. Systems status checks.
44. Pilot transfers to LM.
45. Activate and check out LM systems.
46. CSM and LM separate.
47. Orient LM for descent orbit insertion.
48. Descent orbit insertion.
49. Adjust LM inertial guidance system.
50. LM descent.
51. Landing on moon.
52. Check out LM systems.
53. Explore surface, set up experiments.
54. LM pre-launch checkout.
55. LM's rendezvous radar begins tracking CSM.
56. Liftoff from moon.
57. LM ascent.
58. LM heads into orbit nearly matching that of CSM.
59. LM changes plane of its orbit.
60. LM and CSM fly in tandem.
61. Final rendezvous maneuver begins.
62. Midcourse correction.

63. Rendezvous.
64. CSM and LM dock.
65. Transfer crew and equipment from LM to CSM.
66. CSM and LM separate; LM is jettisoned.
67. Determine transearth injection thrusting requirements.
68. Transearth injection.
69. Systems status checks; eat and sleep period; transmit data to earth.
70. Orient CSM attitude for midcourse correction.
71. First midcourse correction.
72. Systems status checks; eat and sleep periods; transmit data to earth.
73. Adjust CSM inertial guidance system.
74. Orient CSM attitude for midcourse correction.
75. Midcourse correction, if required.
76. System status checks; eat and sleep periods; transmit data to earth.
77. Adjust CSM inertial guidance system.
78. Orient CSM for midcourse correction.
79. Final midcourse correction, if necessary.
80. Adjust CSM inertial guidance system.
81. Orient CSM for separation of command module (CM) and service module (SM).
82. CM and SM separate.
83. Orient CM for re-entry.
84. Re-enter earth's atmosphere.
85. Communications blackout period.
86. Jettison forward heat shield and deploy drogue chute.
87. Deploy main chutes.
88. Splashdown.

*Ullage: A slight acceleration of a rocket vehicle, using special thrusters, to force fuel into engine pump intake lines so main engine can ignite.

SUMMARY OF APOLLO 11 FLIGHT PLAN

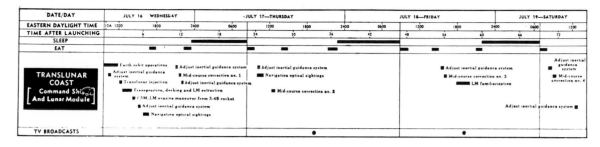

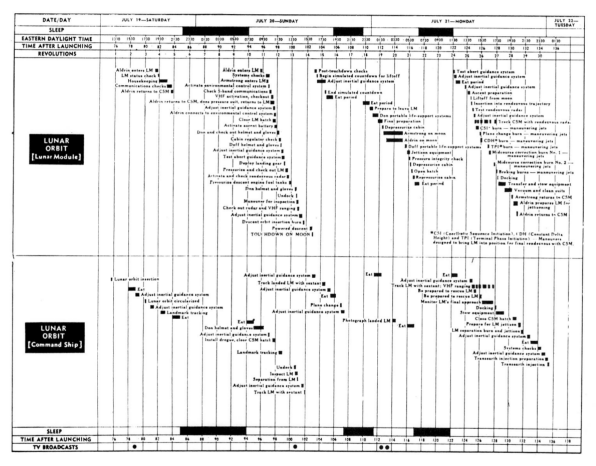

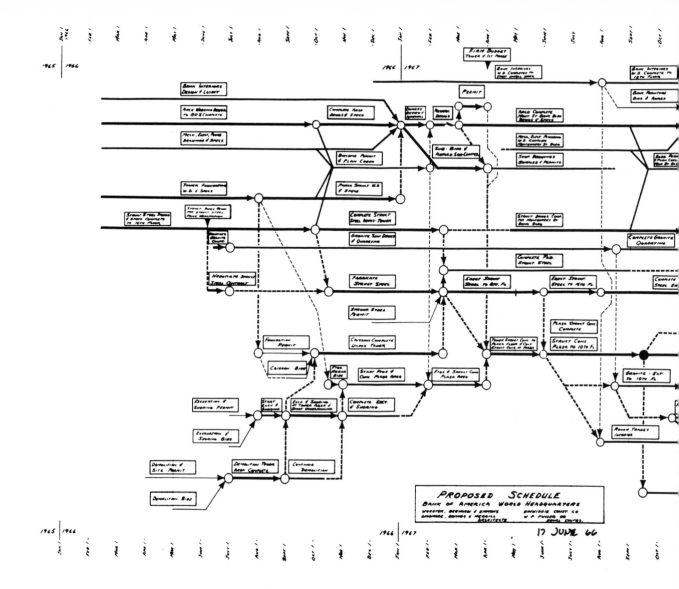

Score for the construction of the World Headquarters of the Bank of America in San Francisco.

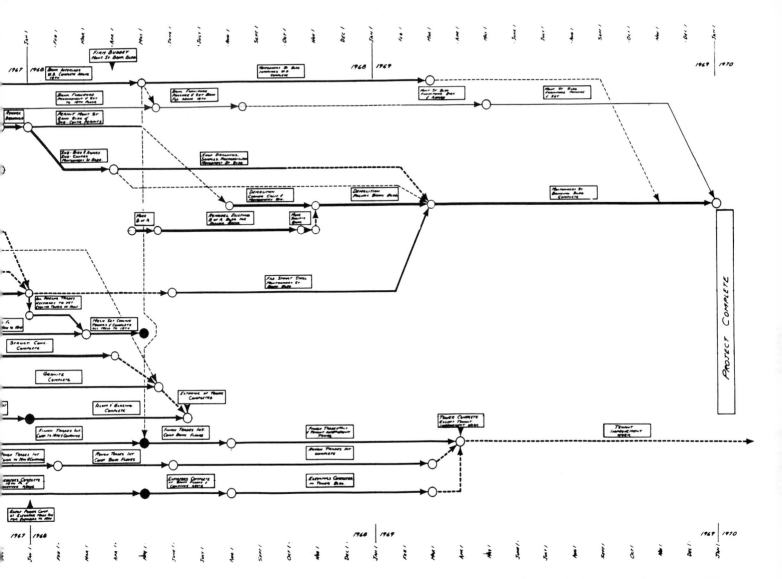

Critical path methods or PERT charts are scores which have been developed in recent years to organize the multiple functions of a complex series of people's activities over time. One use is to program long and involved construction programs. The following figure scores the activity required to construct the new Bank of America building in San Francisco, and plots a great intricacy and variety of activities. This score covers a period of time from January 1, 1966 to January 1, 1970. It commences at the completion of the building-design process and proceeds to score actual construction processes establishing times, sequences, and intersection times of all building trades and elements in the construction process. This score is precise and unipurpose. As little as possible is left to chance; in fact, the major purpose of the score is to eliminate chance as much as possible and predetermine the course of an intricate number of construction activities and events so that materials can be fabricated and delivered to the job site in the proper sequence and at the correct time. It has the great virtue of making visible beforehand to all the people involved what is required of them and when they are expected to start and complete their specific activities. Its relationship to traditional scoring mechanisms for dance, theatre, and music is immediately obvious.

SYSTEM DESIGN FOR METRO CENTER-1985
PERT DIAGRAM

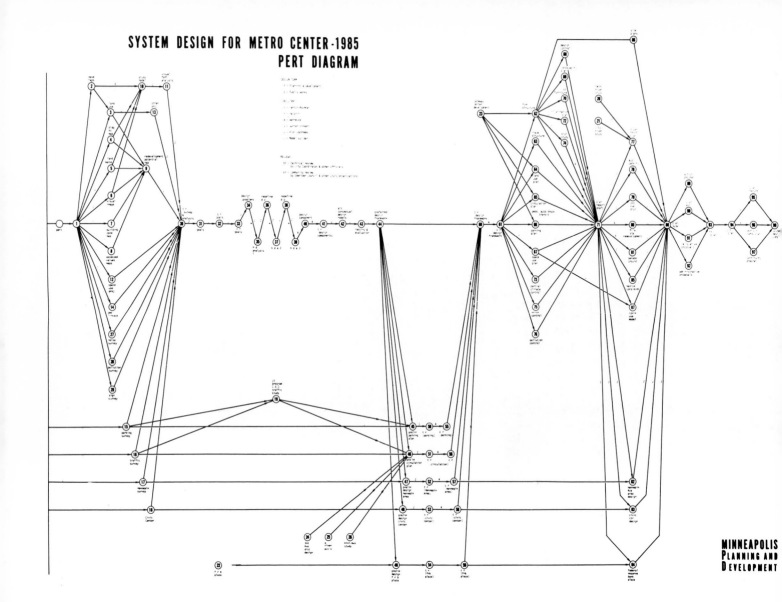

MINNEAPOLIS
PLANNING AND
DEVELOPMENT

More and more planning projects are being PERTed, that is, scored, nowadays. The score enables participants to understand processes and organize for the future. It is significant to point out that Critical Path Method (CPM) charts, particularly, have limited value for scoring innovative work since they imply fixed knowledge of past technologies; they are more "closed" than open scores.

The PERT diagram for a planning program in Minneapolis scores ninety-seven programs and groups of people in the planning process, indicates their interrelatedness, scores start-up and completion dates, and personnel involved over an eighteen-month period. The planning department makes the following statement on the uses of the score:

The preparation of a comprehensive plan and program for development is an extremely complicated and involved process. It requires a systematic approach. It must have the full participation of both public and private sectors of the city. It demands a continuing, creative partnership between government and business.

The Program Evaluation and Review Technique (PERT) has been adopted here as a systematic way to develop the plan. It serves as a tool for coordinating the studies being conducted by city agencies and private consultants. It is an instrument for more effective decision-making on program recommendations.

What follows is a brief description of the various phases of PERT as applied to Downtown Minneapolis. Some are self-explanatory and do not contain any supplemental descriptions. The numbers shown correspond to the numbers of the attached PERT diagram. They are just a guide and the sequence of phases does not necessarily follow in numerical order. At certain points along the path, the different studies come together. These are the important points and the only requirement is that the phases do come together here. These points can be referred to as milestones and are indicated in this description by asterisks. *(Refer to the PERT diagram to see which phases come together at each milestone.)*

"Work Program Comprehensive Development Plan for Central Minneapolis PERT Diagram," (Report) Minneapolis Planning & Development

This score, though similar in technique to the previous construction score, is far more open-ended since many of the programs whose inputs are required are themselves less predetermined. In addition, this is a systematized approach to an *indeterminate* end, and, therefore, has more latitude within the score for variation, chance, and interaction. In this sense it is more like a theatre piece. It, too, possesses the great virtue of visibility. It makes clear, visually, the interrelations of various groups and processes involved in the total-planning process, thus making it possible for each group to see his own position in relation to all the others.

Punched computer tapes are scores
when they serve to guide future
performance of any kind whether
punched by machines such as
computers or by hand. In computer
technology it is the "programming"
portion of the procedure, *i.e.,* the
punched cards fed into the machine
which is usually the score. The
punched tape can either represent R
for a future score or be simply an
inventory item. The tape itself, it
should be clear, has no Valuaction
(V) ability.

place A.M. San Fran	place A.M. Kentfield	place A.M. Kentfield	place A.M. S.F. → S/R	place A.M. Sea Ranch - Gualala Community Center	place A.M. Sea Ranch Gualala Community Center	place A.M. San Ranch	place A.M. Sea Ranch
event CITY MAP	**event** 1- TRAILS MYTH 2. BLINDFOLD WALK	**event** MANIPULATING BODIES ...	**event** TRIP TO SEA RANCH record the environment	**event** MOVEMENT SESSION -Identification with the Sea-	**event** MOVEMENT SESSION	**event** SENSORY WALK - cabin area to Big Cove.	**event** -RITUAL GROUP DRAWING -
assignment start at 11 AM. Follow the city MAP score which was walked in advance to each student. Travel path through the city decided on each scene. UNION SQUARE Car Barn Wool worths	**event** Arrive at 15 Ravine way- assemble on upper terrace. Blindfold group- walks down trontails to a each blindfolded and in silence- Serpents into 3 groups each group do TRAILS MYTH in field space - then led by hidden blindfolded from studio through words to passive experiences environment BEFORE seeing it	Developing skills in handling each others bodies sensitively → work in pairs understanding structural working of the body..... (Session evoked intense emotional experiences)	Start at 6:00 AM in SF. Travel via hwy. 101 → PETALUMA BODEGA BAY hwy 1 along coast AT ½ HOUR INTERVALS - STOP - Record ❶ The environment ❷ Your feelings arrive Halprin cabin @ 12 noon	Passivity - Relaxation Letting Go Following working in groups of 3	Session was cancelled because members of the group came late for breakfast & then stood around.... Leaders used this as opportunity to have discussion about group orientations - processes - responsibility... meaning of lateness	1. Enter the environment and be in it for 2 hours in complete silence - experience by isolating the senses. 2. Free associate - write words with left hand . Share your words describing sensory walk with someone else	Using roll of white wrapping paper -100 yards. group paraded to then arrived and graphically & through naiveté performed a graphic group drawing ritual. Procession back with paper
Mon **1**	Tue **2**	Wed **3**	Thur **4**	Fri **5**	Sat **6**	Sun **7**	Mon **8**
place P.M. San Fran	place P.M. Kentfield -upper terrace-	place P.M. Kentfield	place P.M. Sea Ranch	place P.M Sea Ranch	place P.M. Sea Ranch	place P.M. Sea Ranch	place P.M Sea Ranch
event CITY MAP	**event** 1. GRAPHICS 2. LETTER EVENT.	**event** 1. Assimilate morning experience 2. Lecture - Community Structures	**event** POMO RESERVATION 1- July 4th feast 2- Use - talk in ROUND HOUSE	**event** DRIFTWOOD VILLAGE	**event** DRIFTWOOD VILLAGE 1- DESTROY 2- REBUILD as community Confrontation with Gualalans —	**event** FAMILY DRAWING	**event** -DEPARTURE RITUAL- 1- water - cave offering 2. I AM statements
assignment-continue CITY MAP. cable car Aquatic Park & Pier adapt the attitudes and perform the tasks established on your scene. 5:30 End Journey at YEE JUN restaurant. change places 3 times during the meal - meet members of the workshop	Using brown butcher paper and crayons do a graphic presentation of your experience on the blindfold walk. Share with the group 2- Write a letter to a close friend or family member in which you share your experience of .CITY MAP (This letter and adherence to its internal experience by extrapolating it)	1- Select a person who affected you strongly this AM & describe your reaction to them by working with them for 2 minutes in graphics limited movement 2. PAUL - Lecture to group on the sequences & processes inherent in group development as frame-work for future experiences	afternoon eating talking with Indians, observing Indian rituals in Round house - baseball	June 3 - 5:30 Build a Structure on the Gualala Beach using driftwood & relating to the environment ... in groups or singly as you see fit ...	1. Take down the structures that were built yesterday giving up all structures & a body of finding new 2. Build an Environment as A COMMUNITY after the village was built the group made actual processions (accompanied by drums) through it!	Family graphics - as a community process develop the structure from ideas through drawings - together on large sheets of brown paper - mention your own family member characters throughout - then explain the family. Family evolution - understood the structure thru graphics solely	1- Paper from morning event gathered and an ritual offered to the sea burning at waters edge casting into sea Indian interaction between people about group & their feelings 2- WRITE words about your experience and then put these into sentence using I AM to b
evo Birthday celebration at 521 divisadero St. Performances by: NORMA MUSTILL # Charles Amirkhanian	**evo** Faculty meeting	**evo** Assignment for the Sea Ranch Trip	**evo** Dinner - cook out at Halprin cabin - Shared graphic recording of Trip SF → S.R.	**evo** FIREWORKS EVENT Free time at Kruse Ranch	**evo** Dinner @ Halprin Cabin - discussion of Gualalans accusations & attitudes...	**evo** ECOLOGICAL LECTURE at Sea Ranch barn by Larry → on the Sea Ranch ...	**evo** DINNER AT SEA RANCH RESTAURANT

The above score for a twenty-four-day workshop was used to establish a sequence of activities, and pre-program the major actions of forty student participants in the San Francisco Bay area within a geographical radius of one hundred miles during the summer of 1968. As the sequence of events was linear (that is, the events were sequential and progressive), not overlapping, and all forty people were always engaged in the same basic activities (interactions were confined to those within the group itself), the score has a calendarlike appearance. The major controlling devices within the score, here, are length of time for each event and its location. Each actual event itself admits for great latitude within the time sequence, and the procedures for each event are not significant to the form of the total score (although they had their own internal meanings). This process enabled the workshop leaders to pre-plan an intricate sequence of events in various locations before the fact, and analyze them before, during, and then after the events with an understanding of their interrelatedness. It also made possible adjustments to the program based on feedbacks during the period, with a full understanding of how these adjustments would affect the events to follow. Within the major calendarlike score, other more detailed scores controlled the specific daily events. These varied from happenings to precise theatre pieces and environmental events. (See City Map, p. 79 for a complex and overlapping score for day I.)

Sea Ranch			Kentfield	Kentfield	Kentfield		Kentfield
place A.M.	**place A.M.**	**place A.M.**	**place A.M.**	**place A.M.**	**place A.M.**	**place A.M.**	**place A.M.**
event TOUR OF SEA RANCH TRIP S/R → S.F.	**event**	**event**	**event** MOVEMENT SESSION gravity	**event** MOVEMENT SESSION SPACE LECTURE ·	**event** DAY OF RITUAL	**event**	**event** MOVEMENT SESSION feelings through move

place A.M. events detail:

- **Sea Ranch (Tue 9):** Architectural & planning trip through the Sea Ranch to see buildings · principles. Assignment for trip home: 1. Respond to an event that takes place in the environment. 2. Select an environment & create an event —
- **(Wed 10):** DAY
- **(Thur 11):** prepare for re-entry
- **Kentfield (Fri 12):** — up & down — going with gravity against gravity. falling, lifting, falling into arms. Water games on deck - beginning of buoidity
- **Kentfield (Sat 13):** Back to back → supporting & being supported in open & closed position · · · LARRY - lecture on concepts of space - characteristics of space - changing relation, relationships to movement sessions - near far — To serve as basis for the building of environments
- **Kentfield (Sun 14):** Silent sunrise walk to Phoenix lake and waterfall. Breakfast. Ritual reading of comic strips. group scattered - rest - activities according to need
- **(Mon 15):** DAY
- **Kentfield (Tues 16):** PAUL - Wait - contact source of movement by waiting - move with the source you discover · · · Discussion - feelings about being members of a group. Use the word "I AM" to describe your feelings about the group

Tue 9	**Wed** 10	**Thur** 11	**Fri** 12	**Sat** 13	**Sun** 14	**Mon** 15	**Tues** 16

S/R → S.F.		San Fran	Kentfield	Kentfield	Kentfield		Kentfield
place P.M.	**place P.M.**	**place P.M.**	**place P.M.**	**place P.M.**	**place P.M.**	**place P.M.**	**place P.M.**

place P.M. events detail:

- **(Tue 9):** TRAVEL SEA RANCH ↓ San Francisco
- **(Wed 10):** DAY OF REST
- **(Thur 11): event at 321 Divisadero** 1. DRUM & movement session 2. Report of S/2 → S.F. trip 3. SELF PORTRAITS. — 1. Drumming, chanting & moving to HEART BEAT. 2. Groups report on assignments achieved during trip back - Perform the events which you created as a result of the trip — 3. Make a self portrait using collage materials out out of magazines.
- **(Fri 12):** MOVEMENT SESSION - SPACE. — Move from point → point in space. one by one move directly or indirectly - emphasize spatial qualities.
- **(Sat 13):** BUILDING ENVIRONMENTS — Using the spaces between the ditch → to the gazebo build environments using elements experiment to determine. work in groups or singly. either reinforce or go against gravity. The environment you build will be used.
- **(Sun 14):** DAY OF RITUAL — Silent procession from deck to gazebo. Silent ritual of touch & bathing of hands. Now rituals - poetry, singing, light show, ball playing. Charles Amirkhanian - CONCERT special score for workshop
- **(Mon 15):** DAY OF REST
- **(Tues 16):** Begin GRAPHIC record RECORD KENTFIELD ENVIRONMENT — As an introduction to the graphic recording & score techniques as compositional TOOLS. Record your Kentfield environment: a) Express what you want people to experience. b) Tell what you want. c) Others comment on them. d) Draw accurately, a representation of what you

eve	**eve**	**eve**	**eve**	**eve**	**eve**	**eve**	**eve**

eve events:

- **(Thur 11):** Faculty meeting - evaluation of collage self portraits.
- **(Fri 12):** 1. Lie down & fantasize act out your fantasy 2. Effect of space between people - far & near space.
- **(Sat 13):** ✱ RITUAL CELEBRATION & Banquet --- costumes, ritual supper experience environments at nite - processions - moon viewing — sleep overnite in the environment.
- **(Sun 14):** Faculty meeting
- **(Tues 16):** A.M. DISCUSSION: The Ritual experience as a model for a choreographic method (End with paper masks)

place A.M. Kentfield	place A.M. Kentfield	place A.M. San Fran	place A.M.	place A.M. San Fran	place A.M. San Fran 321 DIVISEDERO	place A.M. San Fran	place A.M. Kentfield
event NAKEDNESS tivate awareness & appreciation of the body — oil bodies - work in pairs Bathe partner Move through the Kentfield environment in nakedness particularly → NET slope woods	**event** MOVEMENT SESSION ① move in straight lines curved lines in threeways ② Break into 2 groups : Build an environment using your own bodies for the other group to move into group 1 - on floor group 2 - Circles Intense reaction to these environments	**event** SKYSCRAPER EVENT 10:30 Perform skyscraper event as you scored it - develop your role & task 3:00 Wells Fargo 450 Sutter Street	**event** D A Y	**event** Free time ... prepare for re-entry	**event** "OUR COMMUNITY" → ↳ Wrote at 321 Divisedero ● WITHOUT leaders ● Wrote comments on paper circles about members of group Started plastic environment in STUDIO 1 Used STUDIO 2 as meeting PLACE	**event** → Meeting & discussion in Women's lounge ◉ Struggle with process Movement Session Began to follow score	**event** MOVEMENT SESSION Structural balance Isolate parts of the body indiv... Re-assemble body Posture alignment MEN'S & WOMEN'S DANCES each group modified others dance through the use of sound ---

Thur **17**	Fri **18**	Sat **19**	Sun **20**	Sun **21**	Mon **22**	Tues **23**	Wed **24**

place P.M. Kentfield	place P.M. Kentfield	place P.M. San Fran		place P.M. Kentfield	place P.M. San Fran	place P.M. San Fran	place P.M San Fran
event NOTATION SYSTEMS - Lectures on notation systems : general principles - various types - applications { Larry to record feelings & personality types { Paul Rainsford, Leary Music - new approaches { Charles - MAKE a Score for a 5 MIN. dance using your own notation system PERFORMANCE : Individual scores notated in the afternoon - select performer in silence - "Score tells everything" here scores of members of group on page & another form of performance!	**event** SKYSCRAPER SCORE • assignment given for skyscraper event ⇨ move between 450 Sutter Wells Fargo AND vertically in the buildings. 1. Develop your own role Score your movement in time & space Assign & develop a task singly or in groups 2 - Draw a master Score for all the above activities ...... **eve** CONTINUE : Performances of Dance scores Prepare for skyscraper event Select costumes & props	**event** SKYSCRAPER EVENT Continue performance until 3:00 4 - 6:30 Meet at studio # describe your role & task and what happened during your event in the skyscraper ✳ Describe your reactions **eve** Free time	**event** O F R E S T	**event** SKYSCRAPER EVENT 1. write script - 2. evaluation - 4-7 arrive at 4 ⇨ write the script that 1-you had developed for the skyscraper event 2-what actually happened 3-Discussion & evaluation ↓ **eve** 1- Finished Dance Scores 2. Continue discussion of skyscraper event - challenges - validity - significance 3- PRESENTED "OUR COMMUNITY" assignment -	**event** OUR COMMUNITY (continued) graphics in Kitchen Discussion of process attempts to develop a MASTER SCORE Pad in KPFA Room Developed outside entrance consider as environment Selected Planning Commission **eve** Meeting of the PLANNING COMMISSION ⇩	**event** ↓ Big meeting STUDIO 2 Bottle as organizing symbol ⇨ HEAVY discussions .... Finish plastic environment STUDIO 1 **eve** SLIDE & LIGHT SHOW ✳ STUDIO 1	**event** 1. GROUP PHOTOGRAPH 2. SELF PORTRAIT CLAY 3. SUMMARY - OUR COMMUNITY 1- group photograph with & without clothes -- 2. Self portrait in clay front three - 20 minute description of portrait using "I AM" statements 3. Leaders - review & summary of the "OUR COMMUNITY" assignment - discuss group **eve** announced weekend about here FAREWELL PARTY ✳

53

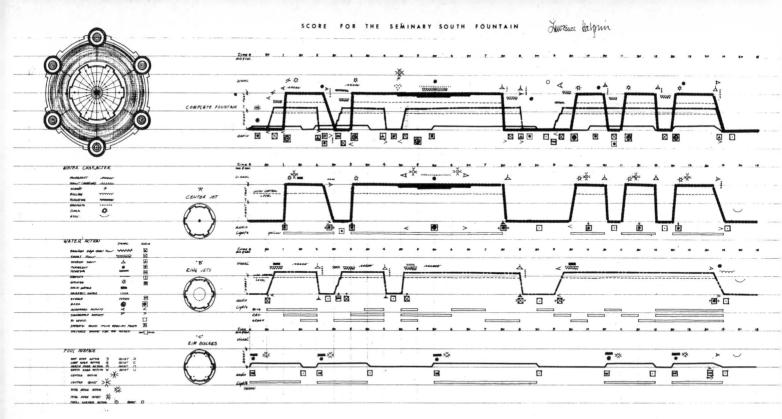

Scores can be used to control physical elements alone, without the interaction of people. What is necessary in order for a score to be useful is motion over time, namely, change. Scores are not of much use in the delineation of static objects where change is not an essential ingredient. Qualities of mobility, however, are difficult to conceptualize or control without scores. For that reason scoring is invaluable in designing, for instance in fountains and water effects, where water, the shapes of water, and their changing characteristics are essential to the design process.

Scores can predetermine and control intricacies of height, jet size, sequence in time, noise (or sound) volumes, and lengths of time and these can be plotted against each other. This scoring technique has proven extremely useful where water sequences an hour or more in length are designed with many different water effects intermingling. Some fountains have been scored with great precision and, in large measure, all the effects predetermined. Others such as the Seattle Center fountain, could not be scored completely since the essence of the design was inherent in the water heads (the performers) themselves. These were agricultural sprinklers set in a predetermined arc, horizontally as well as vertically, as pinwheels. Many of these heads shift direction when counterpressures are exerted, consequently the great delight of this fountain is that it never acts the same twice, since its water effects respond instantly to the countereffects of other water effects, wind, and atmospheric conditions. The score therefore remains open-ended depending on instant feedback, although major control valves for groups of pipes are opened and closed based on the master score.

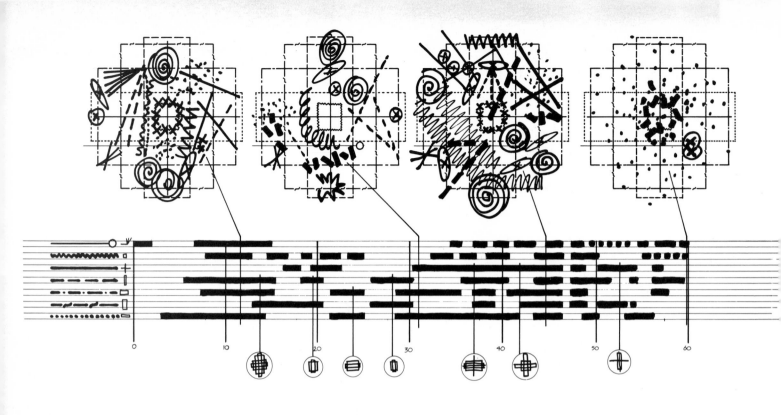

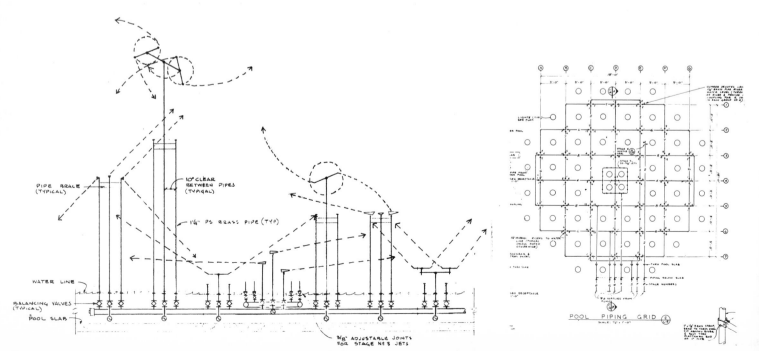

PIPE BRACE
(TYPICAL)

10" CLEAR
BETWEEN PIPES
(TYPICAL)

1'4" PS BRASS PIPE (TYP)

WATER LINE

BALANCING VALVES
(TYPICAL)

POOL SLAB

3/8" ADJUSTABLE JOINTS
FOR STAGE Nº 3 JETS

POOL PIPING GRID

This "score" for the Overhoff-Halprin
fountain at the Seattle Center
notates the process of water effects
over a period of time based on the
piping, water pressures, wind,
timing, gallons per minute, and
special types of heads.

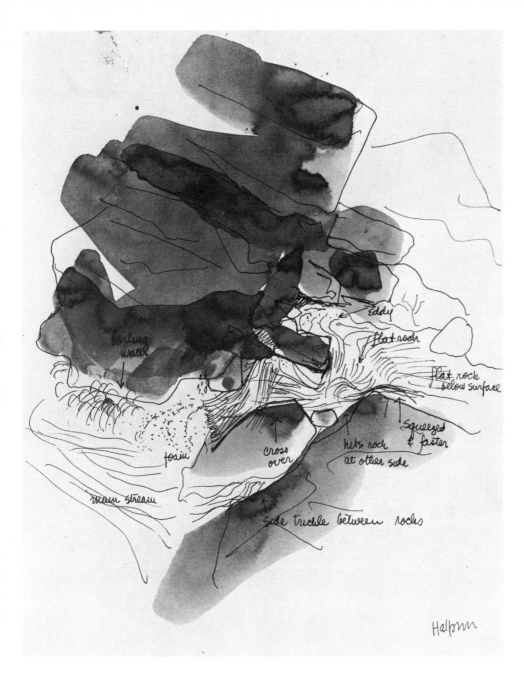

The score for Lovejoy Plaza and Cascade, in Portland, Oregon, resembles the Minneapolis PERT chart superficially, but the two are quite different in intent and purpose. The Portland "score" is a plan form on which six-inch contours in the form of concrete steps were plotted. In this score, the plaza fountain was preconceived by the designers and the exact form and methods of construction were conveyed to the builder and built that way. Water effects were carefully scored into the fountain by studies from nature. First I analyzed the essential qualities of waterfalls in the High Sierra. I observed the effects of constriction on speed of flow; the effects of obstructions and how they break up sheetings of water; the effect of different drops from heights; of sound effects and light qualities; and notated all these in their natural habitat (see sketches). These came under R in the RSVP cycles. From these field observations, I developed scores and then combined them into the final waterfall design which coordinated the structural elements and the water effects into a total composition as Performance (P). Not quite total, however.

The open-ended element remains the people for whom the plaza fountain was designed. The fountain, once built, became, itself, a *score* for movement. The Performance (P) was not an end but a beginning in the cycle again.

Though the environment itself is visually exciting it was conceived as a place for involvement; for physical interaction in which the constructed elements were there to encourage physical and emotional participation by the people of Portland. This is as much a theatre where events can occur, as is a more formalized theatrical environment. I hoped that what we built would stimulate interactions between people and their environment, that they would enter into it and participate in it and with it. I hoped that they would use the water, climb the cascade, wade in the pool, listen to the sounds, and use the entire composition as a giant play sculpture which would heighten and enrich the normal everyday life-activity in the neighborhood. (P) becomes (S). It happened.

This part of the composition was not scored but only implied. The score for people's activities remains open and nonfixed. The composition was unfulfilled until it was occupied.

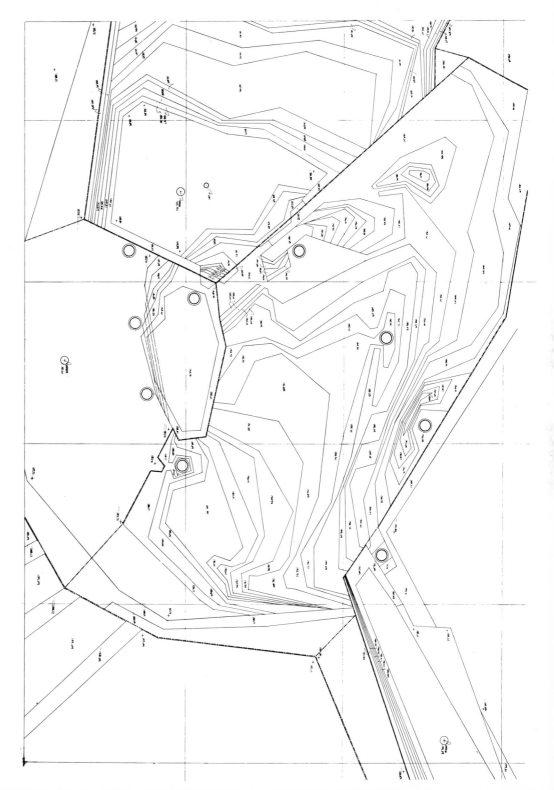

59

In the plaza there should be <u>events</u> .... sculpture shows — concerts — dance events with dancers all over AND arriving to center space from above down stairs around fountain ··· →

Lovejoy Plaza and Cascade,
Portland, Oregon.

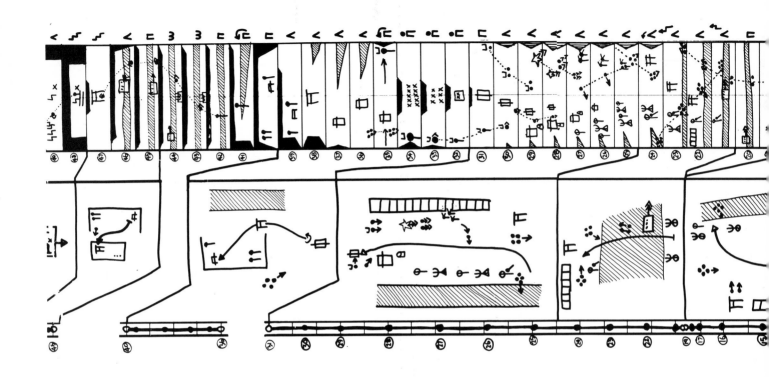

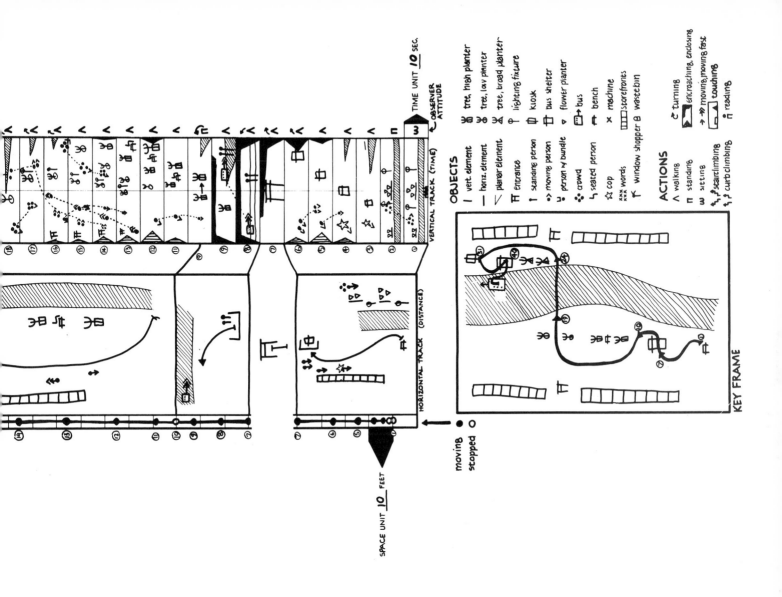

OBJECTS

vert. element	tree, high planter
horiz. element	tree, low planter
planar element	tree, broad planter
entrance	lighting fixture
standing person	kiosk
moving person	bus shelter
person w/ bundle	flower planter
crowd	bus
seated person	bench
cop	machine
xxx words	storefronts
window shopper & wastebin	

ACTIONS

- walking
- standing
- sitting
- stairclimbing
- curbclimbing
- turning
- encroaching, enclosing
- moving, moving fast
- touching
- reading

TIME UNIT **10** SEC.

OBSERVER ATTITUDE

VERTICAL TRACK (TIME)

HORIZONTAL TRACK (DISTANCE)

SPACE UNIT **10** FEET

moving ● stopped ○

KEY FRAME

MOTATION STUDY—
NICOLETT MALL BETWEEN 6th AND 7th STS.

Lawrence Halprin & Associates

Scoring of actual people-motion through space is very complex and has received little attention. Dance notation has concentrated on gesture rather than movement through environments. See figures on Labanotation and Eshkol, pp. 40 and 41.

Navigational plots, of course, have covered ship or aircraft movements in space and time, and fleet movements are covered by scoring devices which, particularly during wartime, control the patrolling and maneuvering and the zigzag patterns of large numbers of vessels as they move in convoys across vast stretches of ocean. But in all these, the relationships between the environment and the motion are fixed, not interrelated. On the one hand we have been able to score motion itself, and on the other hand score for the environment. We have never really been able to correlate the two and devise scores where motion and environments are mutually interrelated and affect each other. Some years ago I became vitally interested in the development of graphic-scoring devices used to design with movement. It appeared to me necessary to break through the idea of the physical environment as fixed and mobility as something else—two polarities as counterforces. I attempted through a system called "motation" to devise a way of scoring which would encourage design for motion. At that time I wrote:

In a world intensely involved in the development of motion through space, little has been done to express it graphically. Movement is all around us; mobility has permeated not only our engineering but our arts as well. High-speed engineering for freeways and rapid-transit systems has become an obvious concern of environmental designers; recently, even sculptors and painters have broken through the barrier of static form, and musicians have dropped their fixations with established

instruments, scales, and positions-on-stage in a search for mobility in space as well as in time. It is imperative that we have a system to express this movement graphically—a tool that will permit us to work with movement itself as an essential and determining element in design.

For some time now, I have been working toward a way of movement notation. In setting myself this task, I assumed that such a system ought to be useful for designers working with pure movement: in dance and theatre; for the newer choreographers whose aim has been to fuse sculpture and painting with theatre; as well as for those of us designing for environment—architects, planners, and landscape architects. This approach to notating movement is a tool that should prove very useful for environmental design, but it was not developed for that purpose alone. I hope it will have universal application for every kind of movement.

Immediate parallels with other explorations in notation come to mind. The most comparable are those in music. Traditionally, music has isolated notes for established instruments and has fixed their positions in space and time on bars, using clefs and variations in note duration. In most cases, the musicians themselves have stayed in one position; only the sound has varied. More recently, musical notation has burst its accepted form, for various reasons comparable to ours. In electronic music, for example, sound is developed, and the resultant tones cannot be scheduled in reference to any fixed system of instruments or notes. The need for new notation arises out of the inability of the traditional approach to express new concepts.

Motation. Environments change their qualities with the variation of speeds they generate. As we move through them, they move around us. On our

freeways and rapid-transit systems, the variation in environmental speed becomes clearer when we observe the contrast in the high-speed foreground and the low-speed background. Sitting at the window of a train, for instance, one gets a certain feeling from passing a series of verticals, a feeling very much determined by their number and the distance between them. Passing piers that are quite close to each other, surprise the passenger again and again with a sense of their nearness. The change of speed is made more apparent in this way, so that, on a route, a pattern of acceleration is soon established. We have all observed telephone poles and track markers alongside a railroad track rush by at great apparent speed while objects on the horizon seem to move hardly at all. As another example, an automobile can be defined as an instrument for moving you to the city, but it can also be defined as a means of moving the city to you. In terms of the individual whose only true continuity is his own awareness, it can be said, with all psychological justice, that the environment moves. This is an essential basis for motation.

"Motation," *Progressive Architecture*

Motation is one way of scoring movement. There are others. What is perhaps most significant is that it is a conception that environments and people can be scored together in a choreography of motion.

Nicollet Avenue in Minneapolis has been scored in this fashion and the score for people-movement through its spaces is illustrated below.

A Japanese design group, involved in the design of the Osaka World's Fair, has applied motation as an analytic tool to the vast central space in the fair, using it as a choreographic tool for fair visitors.

Nicollet Avenue is the major
shopping street in downtown
Minneapolis. Its appearance and
character had been "nondescript,
twentieth-century" (see above photo)
and it was even beginning to lose
the vitality often associated with
ugliness in America. The street was
redesigned to recapture, for
downtown, the liveliness and activity
on the street (at all times of the day
and night) which makes a city
worthwhile being in.

1

INSTRUCTIONS

This sheet indicates the various places you will visit and the path you must travel.

Sheet No. 2 tells you the sequence in which you will visit these places, the time to get there, and how long you are to be at each place. The activities indicated are those you are to perform at each place.

▦ **CABLE CAR BARN**	▦ **AQUATIC PARK**
▨ **WOOLWORTH'S**	**CABLE CAR**
▒ **UNION SQUARE**	**WALK**

The score for a street such as Nicollet Avenue remains a linear experience, just as does the voyage in a car on a freeway for which motation also has been used. But a city downtown area is made up of networks of streets, of areas of shops, plazas, transportation mechanisms, and of people there for a multitude of reasons. The city is a multidimensional space with images full of overlappings and adventures.

This score, called City Map, for a day's events in San Francisco was the first day of a twenty-four-day workshop whose total score appears on page 51. It was a way of introducing students from all over the world to San Francisco, to heighten their awareness of the city and of themselves, and to evoke in them awareness of the city in which they were to spend the next four weeks. It was a score designed to sensitize people to a given environment and to other people's activities within it.

City Map was specially planned so as to allow the forty participants to move on predetermined courses throughout the city without parallelism—that is, each person's track time in each place varied from the next person's, so the group was in constant flux; overlapping and dissolving in each place and never all together, except precisely at 3 P.M. when, in Union Square, all forty participants rose to the sound of chimes and faced the sun.

Along the tracks that each person was given, the score established elapsed time and space, fixed the movement systems to be used, motivated certain attitudes and assigned tasks during the journey. The involvements that inevitably occurred with other people, the adventures, sensitivities, games played, and impressions gained remained unscored and open.

day 1 <u>CITY - MAP</u>

1 - First day is called City Map .. it takes place in San Francisco... Start-up time is 11 AM ... please proceed to your starting point as shown on SHEET 1

2 - GENERAL ATTITUDE (R)
Be as aware of the environment as you can ... This will include all sounds, SMELLS, textures, tactility spaces, confining elements, heights, relation of up & down elements. Also your own sense of movement around you, your encounters with people & the environment AND YOUR FEELINGS !

3 - Union Square is the center of San Francisco - you will radiate to the waterfront, Market St. our major thorofare, Chinatown North Beach our Italian district & the Haight Ashbury...

4 - Other members of our Summer workshop group are following the same "track" as you are but in different sequences... This is a performance and therefore do not speak to any member of the group you may recognize until YEE JUN.

11:00 | 1 | Starting point

12:00

1:00

2:00

3:00

4:00

5:00 | | Finishing point,

Notes on activities

 CABLE CAR BARN

Imagine yourself in a place of fantasies and act accordingly.

 WOOLWORTH'S

Buy a present for yourself and bring it to the birthday party which will take place after dinner.

 UNION SQUARE

1. Share your lunch with somebody.
2. At the sound of the 3 o'clock chimes, stand and face the sun.

 AQUATIC PARK

1. Maintain inner silence.
2. Reflect upon the surroundings.
3. Travel to the end of the pier.

╫╫╫╫╫╫ **CABLE CAR**

Dancers: Look out and pay attention to the drama in the environment.

Architects: Look in and pay attention to drama in the cable car.

 WALK

Don't let anything or anybody touch you. Move quickly and steadily.

○ **YEE JUN RESTAURANT**

Change places three times during the meal.

The master score for City Map (opposite) showing the entire group and its activities. This total score was presented to the group only after the event was finished. During the event itself each individual worked only with his own track (this page). Part of the game was the suspense of knowing that forty other people whom you had not met were traversing the same track.

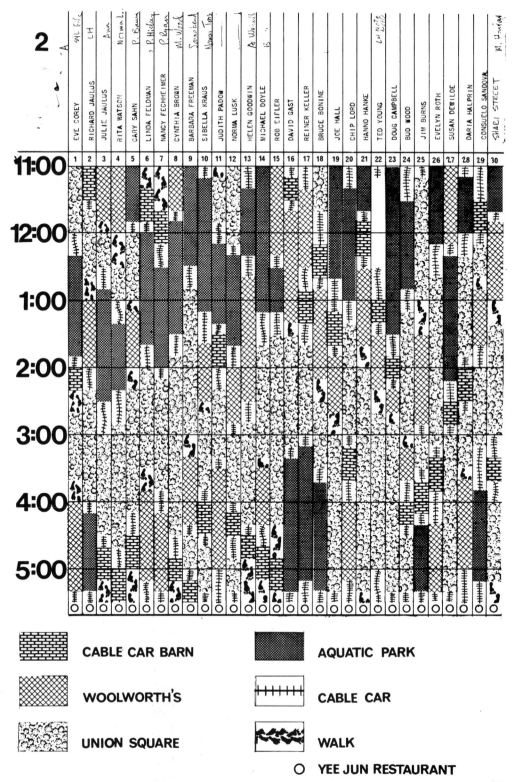

2

EVE COREY	RICHARD JAULUS	JULIE JAULUS	RITA WATSON	GARY SAHN	LINDA FELDMAN	NANCY FECHHEIMER	CYNTHIA BROWN	BARBARA FREEMAN	SIBELLA KRAUS	JUDITH PADOW	NORMA LUSK	HELEN GOODWIN	MICHAEL DOYLE	ROB EIFLER	DAVID GAST	REINER KELLER	BRUCE BONINE	JOE HALL	CHIP LORD	HANNO HANKE	TED YOUNG	DOUG CAMPBELL	BUD WOOD	JIM BURNS	EVELYN ROTH	SUSAN DEWILDE	DARIA HALPRIN	CONSUELO SANDOVAL	SHAEL STREET
1	2	3	4	5	6	7	8	9	10	11	12	13	14	15	16	17	18	19	20	21	22	23	24	25	26	27	28	29	30

11:00
12:00
1:00
2:00
3:00
4:00
5:00

	CABLE CAR BARN		AQUATIC PARK
	WOOLWORTH'S	+++++++	CABLE CAR
	UNION SQUARE		WALK
		O	YEE JUN RESTAURANT

The street configurations of cities are, essentially, a specific kind of scoring device used to guide and control the movement of people. Street configurations are scores because they control not only the patterns and rhythms of people (and vehicles, of course) but also the course, even the nature, of events within a city. It is on the city street that people meet and interact, where they shop, sit in sidewalk cafés, watch girls, court, play games, and roller skate. In most exciting cities the city street conveys the essential qualities of its life and culture, where life and art rub shoulders and in fact become one. Streets sometimes have just happened—as for example Market Street in San Francisco which was born as an on-contour cow track. But more often they have been carefully planned for a purpose. Most often the purpose has been the movement of people along prearranged tracks for service, for religious ceremonies, for regal processions, for defense, for quick access, for many diverse reasons.

As I will point out later, under community scores (p. 151), the conception of streets as scoring devices is a late conception in human communities. Early primitive settlements do not have street patterns; they have only connectors between dwelling units, and tenuous ones at that. These early path connectors arose directly out of Performance (P) without scores, and were "improvisations" which, by constant use, became fixed. As these improvisations became used more and more often, they became woven into the community, more and more buildings grew up alongside them, and the pattern emerged like a happening which has been frozen in time. The pattern of early communities is often extremely random and the linkages between the parts is weak, until community growth forces more than improvisation to be brought into play.

The early patterns of streets, and thus communities, are often likened to the growth of plants or other multicellular organisms which grow by accrual. This is a fallacious analogy. Primitive communities are much more like groupings of animals which come together in a massing of individuals. For example, the nesting patterns of cormorants, which I can observe from my window, are much closer to the patterns of primitive communities than are plant-growth patterns. The birds find an appropriate niche for the nest, but the connectors, the linkages between them, are not significant. Even the random placement of stones dropped by a glacier or some other natural event gives a very clear image of the process of improvisation based on pure Performance (P) by which early communities and their street patterns arose.

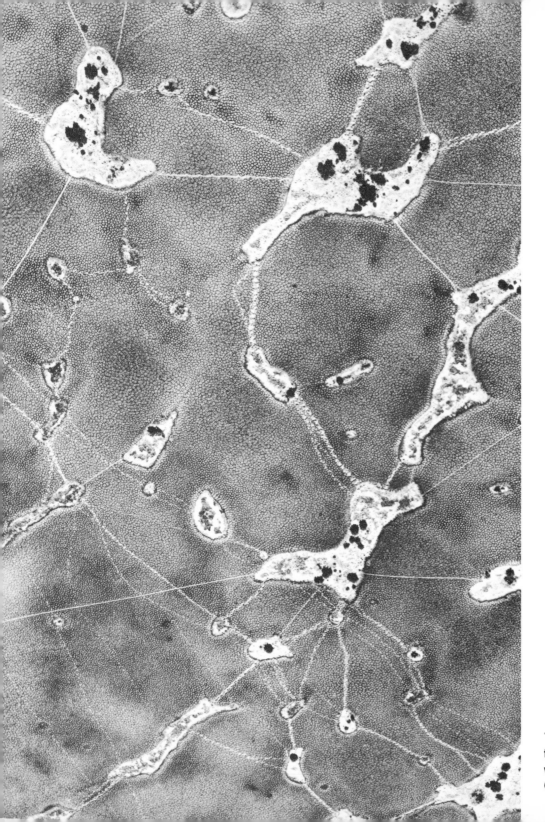

The beginning of the street. Animals' trails connecting various water holes with one another, Dry Lake, California.

As early communities increased in size or were formed under a motivating principle (R) their street pattern had to respond to the need for scoring, and organized patterns based on R, V began to emerge. Immediately, then, the lifestyle on the street changed and Performance (P) became modified.

The diagrams for city-street systems are scores, but the city street *itself* becomes a performance while being created, then a score again (S → P → S). Like scores for theatre or dance, the street score choreographs or controls what happens. The scoring device can establish rigidity and precision or it can encourage interaction in the performance itself. So too for the scores of city streets . . . their patterns and configurations establish the qualities and character of city living not for one performance or several, but for the urban-living patterns for generations to come. Time, over the years, is plotted by the street score against movement and event. More than any other urban pattern the street system scores the quality and character of the life pattern of its inhabitants for centuries.

The movement patterns of urban dwellers start with the city-street pattern and are controlled by it. There is a vast difference between the movement patterns inherent in the grid system so typical of American cities, and the medieval rabbits' warren, or the long vista-terminated Renaissance score, and the freeway score for an automobile-oriented supercity.

The score for each, quite clearly, establishes what can happen—providing certain opportunities and closing-off options. It is important in this context to recognize the score as a multidimensional guiding device—not just a visual one. Most analyses of city streets focus on the enclosing elements, the architecture of facades, and place great emphasis on the visual experience. This is precisely what a score does not do. Scores deal with many facets of human experience including the visual. The implication of scores for city streets is, in fact, that they deal with so many behavior patterns other than visual. This is why some of the most beautiful architecturally-designed streets can be the dullest, and why many streets without any architectural distinction at all can stand out over the years as exciting places to be in. Architecture alone does not make a great street anymore than a fine stage set makes great theatre. The two depend, finally, on what happens and what interactions occur; what they generate in the human experience. Kenzo Tange has said to me: "How do we score an urban street system with its configuration of plazas and openings, its linear patterns and

enclosing spaces? We cannot control in such an environment *all* the elements, because people move randomly and without fixed arrival and departure rates in the spaces." The question is valid, but it has an answer if you understand the nature of scores and the potential they have for openness. The city-street pattern as a score does control certain elements: space, distance, pattern or configuration, mode of movement, and, to a certain extent, rhythm. It does not control with precision many other events except (in a negative way) by exclusion; if sidewalks are four-feet wide they prevent events happening that a thirty-feet wide sidewalk will permit. Sidewalk cafés cannot extend into streets which are too narrow and too full of fumes. The scores for city streets resemble in this sense the scores for *Myths*: they permit

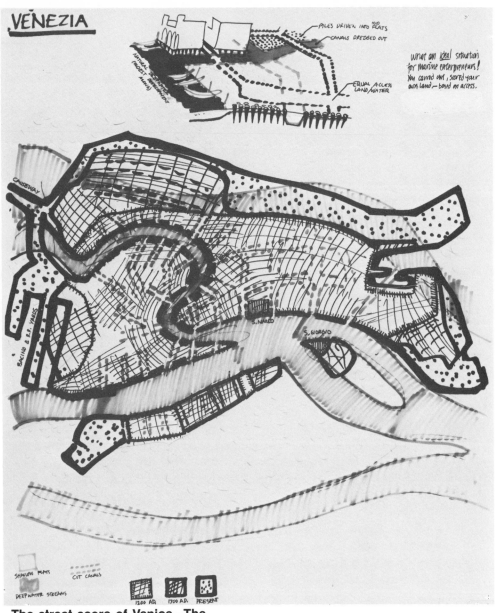

VENEZIA

PILES DRIVEN INTO MUD FLATS
CANALS DREDGED OUT

What an ideal situation for marine entrepreneurs! You carved out, scored your own land — based on access.

NATURAL VEGETATION (FOREST, UNDERGROWTH, MARSH)

EQUAL ACCESS LAND/WATER

CAUSEWAY

BACINO & R.R. YARDS

S. MARCO

S. GIORGIO

SHALLOW FLATS
CUT CANALS
DEEPWATER STREAMS

1200 A.D.   1700 A.D.   PRESENT

The street score of Venice—The Grand Canal, a major freeway for gondolas, snakes through the city. All major access and service is by small side canals. Leisure and quiet is implicit in this street score for a major city whose qualities of serenity and pedestrian spaces have lasted unchanged for centuries. The lifestyle is in direct contrast to Los Angeles.

certain events to happen but what does in fact happen, except during festivals, is unscored. In that sense the city-street score is like the score for a happening—it lines out the environment, the place, the general ambience for events, and then the people create the work of art in the environment.

The influence of the environment is far reaching in this kind of scoring. Just as the events that would emerge from a "happening" on a beach with a group of people is far different from what would happen in a forest with the same group, so does the street score influence the "happenings" of its citizens. The score influences the result. The medium (as McLuhan has said) is the message.

GRID

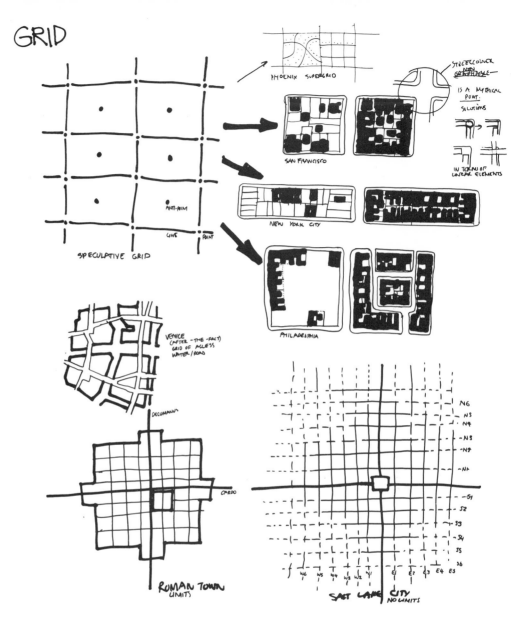

SPECULATIVE GRID

LINE   POINT
ANTI-AIM

PHOENIX SUPERGRID

SAN FRANCISCO

NEW YORK CITY

PHILADELPHIA

STREET CORNER
NOT GRAPHABLE

IS A MYTHICAL POINT.

SOLUTIONS

IN TERMS OF
LINEAR ELEMENTS

VENICE
(AFTER-THE-FACT)
GRID OF ACCESS
WATER/ROAD

DECUMANUS

CARDO

ROMAN TOWN
(LIMITS)

SALT LAKE CITY
NO LIMITS

The impact of the grid on the American lifestyle cannot be overemphasized. It is equidirectional, nonterminated, endless, and transport- rather than pedestrian-oriented. As a score it reflects the energy and noncontemplative characteristic of nineteenth- and early twentieth-century America.

87

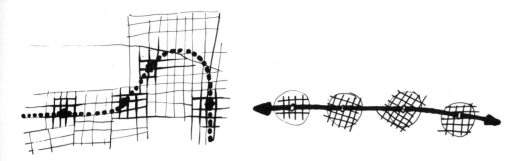

The Montreal Metro. This score for subsurface movement under the grid has established an entirely new lifestyle. Concentration of lively activities occurs at stations underground and a whole new city in effect has emerged under the old.

MONTREAL — TUNNELLING FOR METRO DOESNT DISTURB THE PATTERN ABOVE BUT PRESENTS A BRAND NEW SEQUENCE THROUGH EXISTING NEIGHBORHOODS

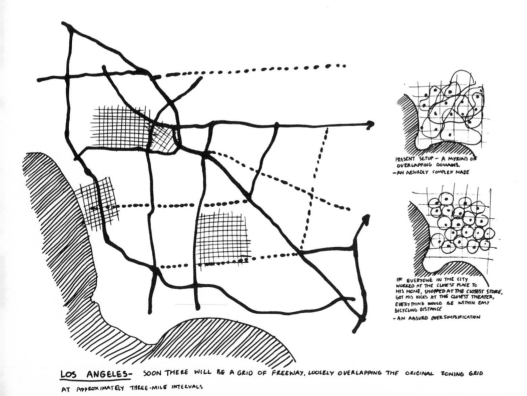

PRESENT SETUP – A MYRIAD OR OVERLAPPING DOMAINS.
—AN ABSURDLY COMPLEX MAZE

IF EVERYONE IN THE CITY WORKED AT THE CLOSEST PLACE TO HIS HOME, SHOPPED AT THE CLOSEST STORE, GOT HIS KICKS AT THE CLOSEST THEATER, EVERYTHING WOULD BE WITHIN EASY BICYCLING DISTANCE
— AN ABSURD OVER SIMPLIFICATION

LOS ANGELES— SOON THERE WILL BE A GRID OF FREEWAY, LOOSELY OVERLAPPING THE ORIGINAL ZONING GRID AT APPROXIMATELY THREE-MILE INTERVALS

The superimposition of a three-mile supergrid of freeways over the old Los Angeles minigrid scores the lifestyle there into a high speed automobile civilization. Speed and mobility is the catchword of this score.

Street patterns influence life patterns and the street score for a city or a village or a new town or a suburb determines the life patterns of its inhabitants. There are other factors in a city which influence the lifestyle, but the streets are a vital and powerful factor in influencing the quality of life in a city and each type of street evokes its own response. This is why city streets are so significant. They affect the quality of the life of their citizens even more than the open spaces in a city. From the presence or absence of noise, pollution, air, and light to the play patterns of the children, their influence is far reaching and subtle. It is, after all, only on streets that people meet face to face, where interaction occurs, where shopping and visiting and eating and festivals occur in cities. It is in the city street in fact that community life is carried on (as distinguished from family and private life) and where, under most cultures, teenagers, young adults, and the old contact each other and carry on their important activities. It is significant to note that once again the street is becoming a meaningful part of our changing cultural patterns and that the young are referring to themselves as "street people." The street *is* the city for many people—only the middle-aged avoid it. For the middle-aged, the home, the security of four walls, the dining-room table and the over-stuffed living-room chair in front of the TV is the city environment. But for all those others, the city street is where the action is and where the quality of life in a city is determined.

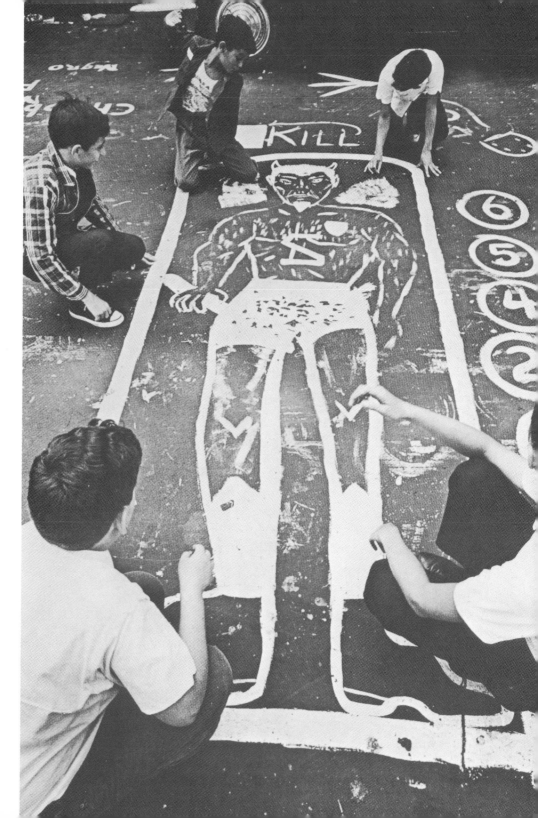

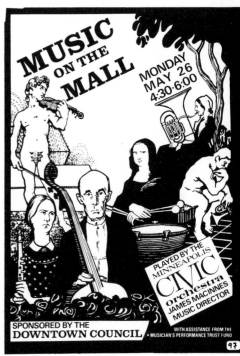

It is on streets that demonstrations occur, where peace marches can happen, where confrontations with the establishment take place. The street has become a place for the theatre of the "Guerrilla Theater," the Dancers' Workshop, and others—as it was in medieval times, part of the life of the community.

I think it important to note that most city designers when confronted with urban problems think of streets exclusively in visual terms, and planar, static ones at that. There is much talk of axes and vistas and termini and massing of buildings and continuity and openings and closing of spaces; there is little discussion of anything else. But the street exists for *activity,* and activity is more than visual. It involves many other senses including the kinesthetic, and, primarily, it involves the *interactions of people* which cannot be prescored.

Parades and Changes performed in the street, Fresno, California. The street can once again become the theatre as it was in medieval times.

A ritual based on street demonstrations. The Dancers' Workshop staged a march, symbolic of protest but without any specific cause. Reactions, interestingly, were as violent as if the marchers were making specific protests. Our times are revolutionary and the symbols of protest against the status quo are the street and the march.

Movement Notation

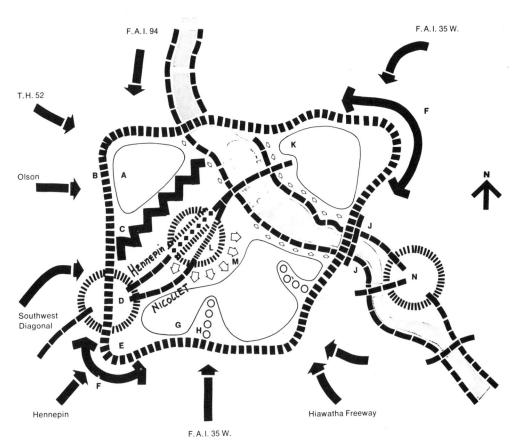

F.A.I. 94

F.A.I. 35 W.

T.H. 52

Olson

F

B A

K

N

C

Hennepin

L

M

J

J

D

Nicollet

G H

E

Southwest
Diagonal

F

Hennepin

F.A.I. 35 W.

Hiawatha Freeway

A General Industrial Use
B Freeway Loop
C Railway Barrier
D Park
E Tunnel
F No Direct Access from Freeway
G Mixed Light Industrial, Residential and
   Convention Activities
H General Industrial/Residential and Mixed
   Commercial Use
J Desired Pedestrian Routes
K Mixed Industrial/Residential and
   Commercial Use
L City Centre
M City Centre Expansion
N University

The street score can open
possibilities, it can make things
available, it can energize the
potentiality of events. That is what
the scoring for city streets should
concern itself with.

The movement notation figure is a
"scoring" analysis of the various
types of streets in Minneapolis,
Minnesota. Each type is indicated by
a different graphic representation,
and each evokes a different kind of
lifestyle from the sixty-five-m.p.h.-
car-only-oriented freeway loop to the
newly pedestrian-oriented leisurely
Nicollet Avenue.

The score for city streets is, of
course, multidimensional.
Graphically, in plan, the impact is
one of a two-dimensional, simple
planar pattern. Street scores have
usually been drawn that way and
have had all the weaknesses
inherent in this limitation.
Topography was rarely taken into
account—often with disastrous
results. On some occasions,
however, the error has produced
chance effects of great beauty, as in
San Francisco where the ubiquitous
grid, running wild up and down the
hills willy-nilly, provided magnificent
open views down steep slopes
toward the bay. Here the score
created effects which it was never
intended to do.

The three-dimensional requirement
of street scores imposes concerns
for the passage of time as well as
space. Streets scored centuries ago
when structural systems of wood and
masonry limited the heights and
cornice lines of buildings along the
street are now giving way to
increasing change vertically. Old

scores for streets are confronted with new series of "chance" occurrences, not envisioned when the scores were drawn. The chance occurrence has to do with new heights of buildings inserted among the old, each decade bringing its own new scale and its own new heights along the old street.

The question that faces us in many old cities whose street scores were not developed with vertical "chance" in mind is whether, now, to try to control heights through new scoring devices imposed over the old scores. There is pressure both ways. The greatest pressure, of course, comes from developers who wish to build as high as possible in order to squeeze as much economic return out of a parcel of land as possible. That is putting undue emphasis on economic return as just one element in the score. On the other hand, many designers resist the new scoring on the assumption that, as with other types of human activity, "chance" will produce better results than control. Others maintain that there are issues at stake which cannot be left to chance, and therefore the new developments should be rigidly scored. They point out (and I am among them) that ecological and biological needs must be met—that these cannot be left to chance because they are too self-evident and too important and that they must control the scoring systems. These biologic determinants are light and air and sun and microclimate and views.

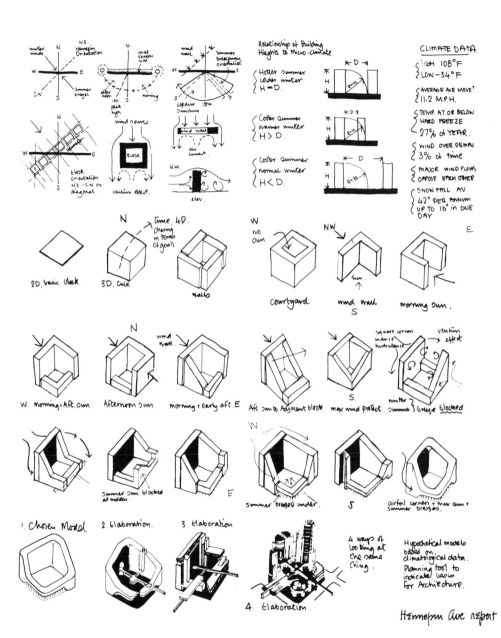

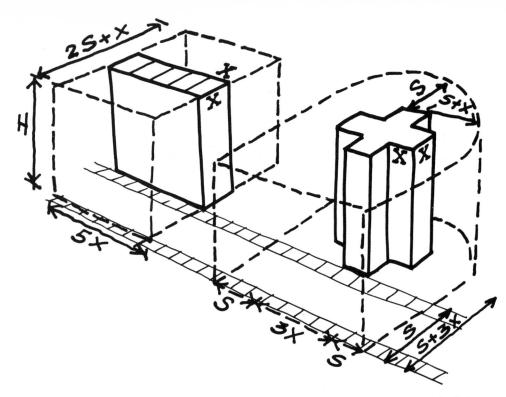

The form of a building has an enormous impact on the street score. It influences open space around it as well as its relationship to adjacent buildings. The dotted lines represent the approximate volumes required by each form to function in relation to its own space and adjacent buildings. To apply the formula use S = 100, H = 100, X = 5. Then the area for the linear equals 62,500 square feet and the area for the cruciform equals 103,200 square feet.

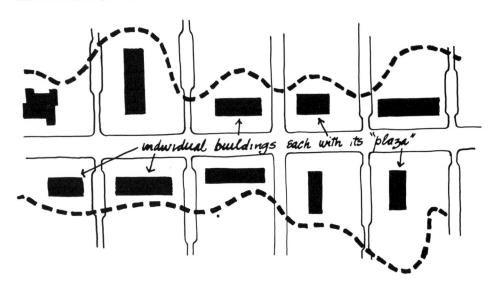

individual buildings each with its "plaza"

Zoning affects the street score. In New York City the "open space ratio" provision of the ordinance stipulated that each building must provide its own open space "on its own property." The result has completely changed the look and feel of New York because it has forced a series of towers each on its own plaza. On the face of it this may sound like a good idea but it has destroyed the visual "continuity and order of the street" and prevented aggregations of open space to produce major plazas.

If these biologic needs are to be met they must become part of the new street scoring. Heights of buildings, open spaces, and views need to be taken into consideration before scoring begins. These inventory items are part of Resources (R) and form the very basis for a human environment. The nonrigidity of the score is a creative act which must be maintained. But the flexibility and noncontrol desirable within the scoring process itself cannot be allowed to destroy the matrix of the community environment within a city. It is precisely here that R, V in the RSVP cycles must be brought into play, in order to set selective limits on the short-term results with a view to scoring for the benefit of the whole community and its ecological needs. Attempts have been made in many cities in this direction. Floor-area ratios which score heights of buildings against land coverage is a common solution; but this device has severe drawbacks. In itself, it can force height into cities, and create building setbacks which affect adversely the character and quality of the street. In addition, this method of scoring is developed on a parcel by parcel basis rather than a complete, city-wide street basis, and thus has been unable to properly score entire street configurations as it should. It is as though a whole dance were scored, using only the gestures of each separate dancer—allowing the environment to emerge from the gestures.

The only city in the United States which has scored its entire street pattern in three dimensions is Washington, D.C., where the horizontal configuration has been extended to the vertical. One hundred and ten feet above sea level has been a uniformly established height above which no building in the city can extend. The breakdown of this score can be seen across the river in Rosslyn where height restrictions no longer apply and a kind of glassy chaos has resulted. The negative quality of this controlling scoring technique is very apparent, for Washington is an extremely dull city indeed. To overcome this dullness and yet maintain a three-dimensional order, studies have been made by Chloethiel Smith of ways to penetrate the vertical envelope through prescored enabling devices, but the system has, so far, not been accepted.

The new movement systems for cities generate increasingly complex possibilities and experiences. They must be conceived to have potentials that extend to all kinds of sensory awareness and which should be scored in. Movement in tall buildings can be more than simply a way to get from the lobby to the thirty-fifth floor with Muzak. The potential for accomplishing more than that in the human experience has not yet even been explored. For that reason we "scored" a skyscraper event in one of our environmental workshops which used several skyscrapers and their elevators as part of the choreography of the event.

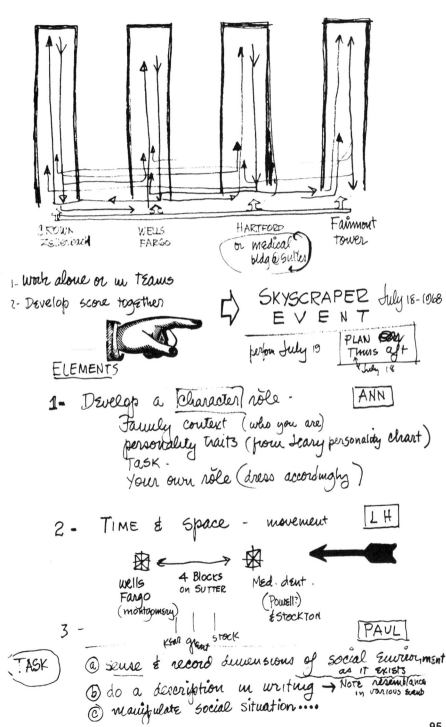

Preliminary score for a skyscraper event, 1968 Halprin Summer Workshop. The score involved the movement of forty participants up and down in the elevators of several San Francisco skyscrapers and movement on the streets between them. In addition to the purely movement experience, workshop members also assumed specific character roles involving tasks to be performed within the buildings.

The potential for scoring and designing urban-movement systems at many levels and speeds, with human experience as an essential ingredient in the score, is one of the unexplored facets of urban design for the future. I can conceive scores which will integrate all kinds of movement in cities from subway systems to plazas to parks to vertical elevators to bridges between buildings—all scored for events to happen and for people to enjoy. One of the few times I have ever even contacted this kind of attitude was in Montreal during Expo '67, when the progression from subway to train to minirail and finally entering into the U.S. Pavilion via minirail became an exciting and wonderful series of experiences.

The newer scores for sections of older cities now under redevelopment and renewal have *had* to cope with dimensions beyond those of the earlier streets. Now additional dimensional conceptualizing is mandatory in response to the demands placed on the modern street. New scores must be developed which can control and separate disparate movement systems: cars from pedestrians; mass transit; parking for automobiles; and pedestrian-movement systems of different kinds—both vertical and horizontal. The scores for each one of these systems can be developed separately and then coordinated with the structural scores for building locations and heights into a master score, which like a music score for many instruments coordinates and orchestrates the various elements together.

The master score for an urban downtown area depends heavily on this kind of integration of street-movement systems and buildings, combining, as it does, open and closed spaces, corridors of movement, both horizontal and vertical, and the closed spaces required for working and living. Urban systems increasingly attempt to coordinate these various elements into a master score rather than a master plan. The Yerba Buena Center plan is basically such a score because it establishes spaces, three-dimensional corridors for movement, and elements of function, but does not preclude change or the vagaries of chance over time. Complete rigidity and control have given way to a line of action. Some elements are "designed into" the score, but others are purposely left open for other hands and other times to develop.

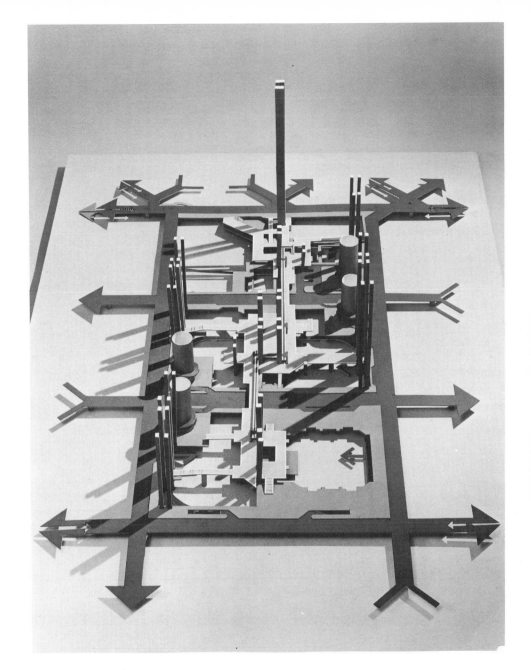

The three-dimensional movement
score for Yerba Buena Center, a
thirty-five-acre area to be
redeveloped in San Francisco. The
score based itself on movement
elements which include: the new Bay
Area Rapid Transit underground
subway concourse, several
pedestrian levels, parking for four
thousand cars, an
airline-terminal-service access for a
major convention and exhibition
center, aerial moving sidewalks,
vertical spiral garage ramps, and
elevator clusters. These are the
dominant elements in the score.

The natural environment is the physical matrix for human communities, so it is important to discover *why* it is, *what* it is, and the *how* of its developing that way. I have called this ecoscoring.

Ecoscores are ways of describing, through notations, the way natural configurations developed over a period of time. They are ways of indicating the on-going process of development by which natural events will continue to proceed. Ecoscores are important to ecosystem description because the science of ecology is a *science of process,* and that in ecology what is significant is not so much the understanding of what exists at any given moment in time, but that the existence is ephemeral and in constant motion, constant change.

The value of ecoscores is that they make visible the consequences of action. Fraser Darling has said, "The practical value of ecology is the ability to forecast consequences of certain courses of action and of observable trends." ("The Ecological Approach to the Social Sciences," *The Subversive Science,* Paul Shepard and Daniel McKinley, editors.)

The science of ecology, which is the study of organisms' relationship to their environment and all other organisms, has become all encompassing and in my view very rightly so. It bears the same relationship to the other biological sciences as Gestalt psychology does to the other psychologies, in that it deals with relationships between things as much as with the things themselves. The two are in fact very related and complement each other;

98

ecology dealing with the physical world and Gestalt psychology with the emotional world. But they are both existential and base themselves on the importance of process and growth and change in what exists—not some mythical idealized world.

We have gotten ourselves (as White and others have pointed out) in deep trouble ecologically, largely because of our Judeo-Christian religious morality which has been anti-ecologic. The essence of this morality is that man is *not* part of nature but preordained to dominate nature:

God planned all of this specifically for man's benefit and rule; no item in the physical creation had any purpose save to serve man's purposes. And, although man's body is made of clay, he is not simply part of nature; he is made in God's image.

Lynn White, Jr., "The Historical Roots of Our Ecological Crisis," *The Subversive Science,* Paul Shepard and Daniel McKinley, editors

In fact, the story of the creation as reported in the Bible is an anti-ecologic score. And (except for Franciscanism), "Christianity . . . not only established a dualism of man and nature, but also insisted that it is God's will that man exploit nature for his proper ends" (White, *The Subversive Science*). It is also a scoring idea which had perhaps great validity at a time when paganism gave permission for licentiousness and religion was a cloak for venality. But its later implications were unforeseen.

Paganism, on the other hand, was *positively* ecological and saw man as part of, almost subservient to, nature. This is also true in most Eastern religions.

In antiquity, every tree, every spring, every stream, every hill had its own "genius loci," its guardian spirit. . . . Before one cut a tree, mined a mountain, or dammed a brook it was important to placate the spirit in charge of that particular situation and to keep it placated. By destroying pagan animism, Christianity made it possible to exploit nature in a mood of indifference to the feelings of natural objects. The whole concept of the sacred grove is alien to Christianity and to the ethos of the West. For nearly 2 millennia, Christian missionaries have been chopping down sacred groves which are idolatrous because they assume spirit in nature.

Lynn White, Jr., "The Historical Roots of Our Ecological Crisis," *The Subversive Science,* Paul Shepard and Daniel McKinley, editors

No wonder that the combination of this ethos and the ethos of private-property-for-gain has rapidly deflowered the earth.

As a result of this Biblical score, man has worked unilaterally in a linear progression, believing always in the ultimate validity and even sanctity of his own limited aims, dependent on technology as servant, in himself as God on earth, and in progress as always fruitful.

We have begun, increasingly, to reap

the consequences of these attitudes in the polluted, overpopulated, ugly environment which we have built for ourselves.

A new ethic is needed—an ecologic ethic—perhaps born of knowledgeable self-interest, one which recognizes ourselves, once again, as part of nature. One which understands that, if we violate much longer our ecologic ethic we will have started so many processes in an irreversible direction that normal homeostatic safety valves will no longer operate, and the earth as a viable place with any qualities which make it worthwhile to live in will no longer exist. This ethic needs to operate as a new force to see man in nature, integrated, by which actions are based on a worldwide understanding of the ecologic score-as-process, and the implications of these actions clearly understood. We need an ecologic "bill-of-rights" to establish reverence for the inherent process of nature's own system.

Tohru Takemitsu—"I recognize of the notation as the same sort of phenomenon as the growth of the constellation or a plant. There, important is, changes that is not perceived directly visually" (*Notations,* John Cage).

In the planning of regions or areas of larger or smaller geographical units, ecological scoring is a way of understanding processes and the inherent characteristics and values of land—it is a mechanism for making visible the nature and characteristics of natural communities.

the biblical creation score

The score has had an incredible effect on 4000 5730 years of human history since it was written .... Here is a case where the score documented a process in the past .. has made a massive effect for centuries and will continue to do so for the future — unless it is unmasked for what it is ... A Planning effort TO CONTROL

score	effect
1- God worked for 6 days	1- Work is god-like - we work all week ....
2- god rested on the 7th day	2- we rest one day of the week but only as "a reward"
3- 7 Day creation period	3- our lives broken down into weekly rhythms.
4- GOD created man	4- Direct relation god → man NOT evolved but arose full blown
5- Woman made as companion from man's rib	5- Subsidiary position of woman
6- Man created in GOD's image	6- Man god-like. more significant than other organisms
7- Man "named" animals	7- Man "better than" & dominant over animals
8- Man originally in Garden-of-Eden	8- Man was at first part of Nature
9- Serpent tempted man with the apple	9- Nature itself is a temptation
10- When Man ate of the tree of knowledge he was expelled from "the Garden" of Eden	10- With knowledge (and responsibility) comes a rejection of a simple direct relationship to nature
11- Man told to populate the Earth.	11- Man has the responsibility to rule & populate the Earth for his own sake.
12- GOD made man cover his nakedness as punishment for acquiring knowledge.	12- Concept of original Sin & the Evil of "natural sensory reactions"

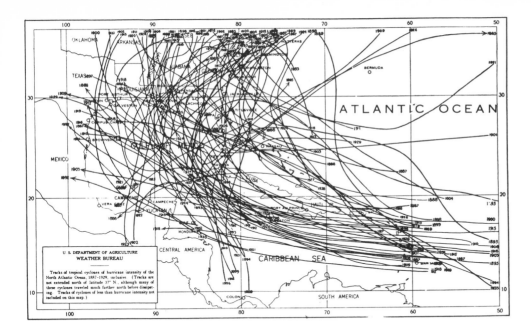

Score of tropical hurricanes in the North Atlantic during the period of 1887-1929—a record of ecological occurrences over time. The patterns of the score can be a guide for the future.

The land itself has scoring mechanisms built into its physical characteristics. Through lengthy processes, these have evolved into recognizable parts which are identifiable and quantifiable. They have to do with elements in the land, such as soil types, vegetative cover, drainage patterns, aquifers, wind and rain patterns and quantities, and so forth. The scores which notate these factors are natural, in that they derive from natural causes: for example, earthquake faults are scores which characterize the pattern of faulting lines within a region reflecting deep tensions within the bedrock. These fault scores were not only operative in the past, but prognosticate the future; they are clear "lines of action" telling not only what has transpired in the past but also what may be anticipated in the future. The inevitability of this kind of score has to do with *what* will happen. Precisely when and to what degree and how is never quite clear from the score, and the effect of future faulting depends in large measure on how its messages are read and what use is made of the score. The scores are clear; what they have to say is also clear. But, as with any score, the feedback and use and interpretation of the implications of the score depend entirely on the people "reading" the score and their commitment to deal with the implications of the score. Scores tell what and why, but they leave the "how" up to the individual.

The earthquake-fault score is a very dramatic example of the scoring inherent in the earth. It is also very precise when understood. For example, the studies on both sides of the earthquake fault at the new town of Hamilton indicate that one hundred feet on both sides of the fault trace must be kept open.

Tidal patterns for San Francisco. An ecoscore affecting all aspects of marine life.

The earthquake score, however, can be ignored. It has been largely ignored in the San Francisco Bay area with disastrous results in 1906 and potentially disastrous results sometime in the future—when, we do not know. Just at this writing, a major earthquake has occurred in Santa Rosa, predicted as a future epicenter of activity.

Other nature-scoring mechanisms are less dramatic but nonetheless clear. Land-soil types score what can be built upon them in terms of weights of structure. They also score drainage patterns, flood potential, and so forth.

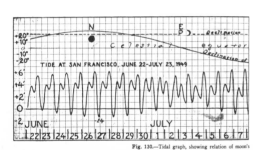
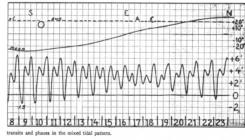

Fig. 130.—Tidal graph, showing relation of moon's transits and phases in the mixed tidal pattern.

Scores for wind indicate what can be anticipated in an area in the future. Vegetation not only scores itself but scores the complex interrelationships of a site, and is an "indicator" of many intricate and interwoven factors: soil type, wind, acidity and alkalinity, and so forth.

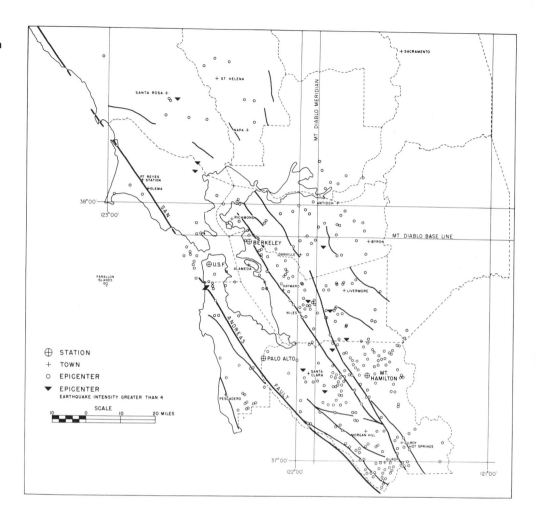

San Francisco Bay Area earthquake fault lines. These notate both past processes and are scores for the future quakes which may be anticipated. As this caption was being written a major quake occurred in Northern California with a 5.6 Richter reading causing severe damage in Santa Rosa, noted on the chart as an epicenter.

The score applied to the design of Hamilton, a "new town" projected near San Jose. The score indicates the area which will be influenced by future quakes and the zone within which no public buildings such as schools may be built.

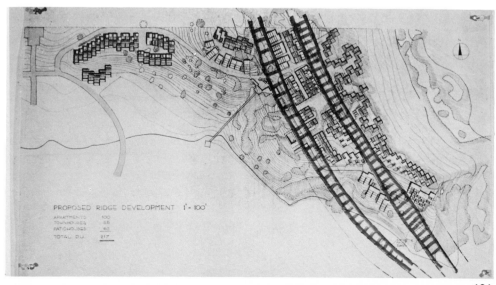

PROPOSED RIDGE DEVELOPMENT 1"-100'

The relationships between the various elements in the score become more involved, more complex, and more interrelationships emerge as one studies and empathizes with the scores of nature. Eventually they are understood to form a complete and intricate orchestration of notes and melodies, each carrying a message of its own but combined into a symphonic totality which biologists call an ecosystem. The ecosystem is a unique combination of all the elements in an area at a particular moment in time, each one of which has its own unique characteristics and its own individuality but which together form another organism which is not only the sum of all the individual, but becomes more than just a sum. The community becomes a total individual itself. Thus, an ecosystem is a community made up of all the plants and animals and land and soil and wind and climate within a place—each interacting with the other and forming more than the parts.

It is perhaps significant here to explain the concept of *climax* in ecosystems. Our planet started, as we all know, barren of soil but composed of rock areas and water areas. Perhaps most prototypical now are the high glaciated areas in mountainous regions such as the High Sierra. Starting with a series of successional stages, simple organisms (called pioneers) like lichens acting upon the rock faces dissolved the rock into soil, which then washed down into the small valleys making them, then, available as a place for other plants to grow, which in turn made it possible for animals and insects and a whole

range of organisms to populate the area. The plants and animals in the habitat keep on shifting and modifying the habitat in a series of successions, each more stable than the last, until finally (usually after eons of time) the successions become stabilized. Successions do not occur at any given or average rate of speed, but they do eventually result in a community of plants and animals whose composition is relatively—in an evolutionary sense—unchanging (or stable). The community works to exclude new species from becoming established within it and, barring a disaster such as disease or a major climatic change or other major positive shifts, will develop into an increasingly stable form as individuals tend to be replaced by their own progeny. This is called a climax community.

The relationship between ecosystems as a biological manifestation and the approaches of the Gestalt psychology are evident and important. Gestalt psychology deals with processes as important to what *is*. It investigates relationships and the foreground-background concept involving the organism within his environment, not separable from it. It looks at structures as the resultant of how they developed; not some imposed image of why they should have happened. The two "ologies," therefore, are existential and closely related in a positive and life-oriented way. What is also important is, to reiterate, that ecosystems derive *from* and are *in* process. They are never completely static, since all parts are always in interaction. They *do* arrive at balance. But this, in point of geologic time, is only momentary. If any element within an ecosystem is changed or varied, the whole system changes. And these changes cannot with any degree of assurance be prognosticated. The urban community is now quite clearly into such a major ecosystem shift, which seems to me to be a major positive shift in our succession, but has a long way to go to achieve "balance." One can "score" new elements into an ecosystem but what emerges cannot be controlled or completely anticipated from the score.

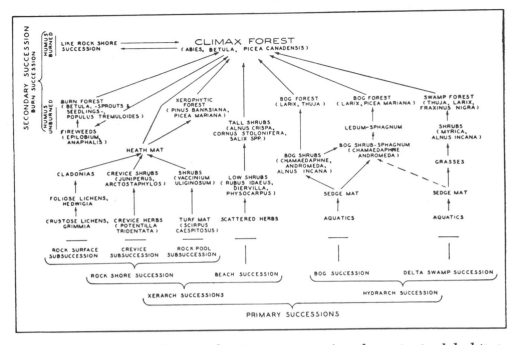

A diagram of the trends of succession for the principal habitats

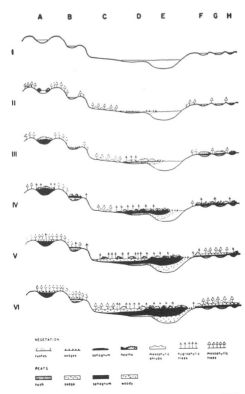

Two diagrams which describe succession in ecosystems. The Laurentian Shield diagrams the evolutionary progression from lake to sphagnum bog and explains a process very similar to that illustrated in the High Sierra although the plant species themselves differ. The upper diagram is a successional story for an entire region in Lake Superior.

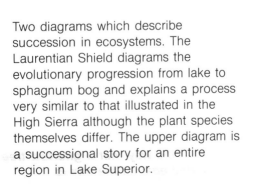

Process and Form—The Gardens of the High Sierra

"The Arretes violently upwarped a million years ago are made up of granite which vary in color from gray to pink and from speckled to white. Up high above timber line the lichens, earliest pioneers, dissolve the rock into tiny beginnings of soil which fill the split rock crevasses and form footholds for the later alpine flowers. As the water from melting snows rushes down the slopes it carries the soil into the small tarns, they fill gradually, and slowly planting invades the water. As time passes the tarn changes into a grassy pond garden—shallower, more planted, softer in outline—the rocks and boulder islands become covered and less distinguishable. Hummocks of grass invade the water—often dikes of soil create different levels in the garden and the forms and shapes of the grassy humps take on the soft interwoven curvilinear shapes of water. It is a garden of movement in static form, whose outlines imply movement and the processes of change. It is a miniature landscape, boggy underfoot, whose surfaces undulate slightly vertically as well as horizontally, and whose scale is deceptive and unreal. These are gardens which could be relief maps of the world seen from great heights or swamplands at the headwaters of rivers. In fact, they are stages in the development of meadow gardens and intermediate in quality and character between the tarn garden and the meadow garden. The Miro-esque shapes, the interrupted, quietly reflective surfaces of the water, the textural qualities of the grassy verges, gives this garden a unique quality reminiscent of abstract paintings.

"The rocks and sculptured forms of granite have in fact been 'placed' by the glacier—the shapes of the meandering stream beds have been carved by their waters and the dwarf trees are marvelously shaped by the action of wind and snow. Violent forces have put these gardens together. And as one sits amongst them—with their poised quality of delicately balanced natural elements, they are experienced as great works of beauty because they are profound expressions of natural processes.

"Up there above timber line, among these gardens whose design has been fixed by natural phenomena, we can watch in action the sources of our own aesthetics. Here are the raw materials on which we base our sense of art organization—here is the reference point of our designs, our sense of order, the sculpture to which we refer in our mind's eye, the colors we see as being right in juxtapositions we enjoy. And above all here, in clear view, are the very processes by which these orders, these arrangements in space, these sculptured forms are created.

"Nature has many lessons for us, but to me, as a designer, these two are most important. The first of these is that order, natural order, is overwhelmingly clear and that I relate to it easily and organically and my own sense of order derives from it. Order in this meaning does not imply the picturesque qualities of scenes in the way that a gnarled tree silhouetted against the sky is picturesque. This order has to do with process—it has to do with natural rhythms, of qualities of relationships between objects; of lightness and heaviness; of the sense of gravity and the density of rock, of energy and force.

"Second is process. Here is clearly seen the way in which our sense of nature arises. Process and product become synonymous and the sequence of events is absolutely clear. Art is here evolved, by the inevitability that natural chance brings. The forces of natural phenomena have their own internal logic.

"In the design of our environment we can strive for this same sense of inevitability through processes which can use chance and accident selectively.

"Naturalism, natural senses of order, natural materials, natural landscapes and gardens, natural cities and towns and urban spaces can arise not through copying nature's pictures but by using her tools of composition. Naturalism in its true meaning is when process and product are the same."

Lawrence Halprin
Landscape, Winter, 1961–62

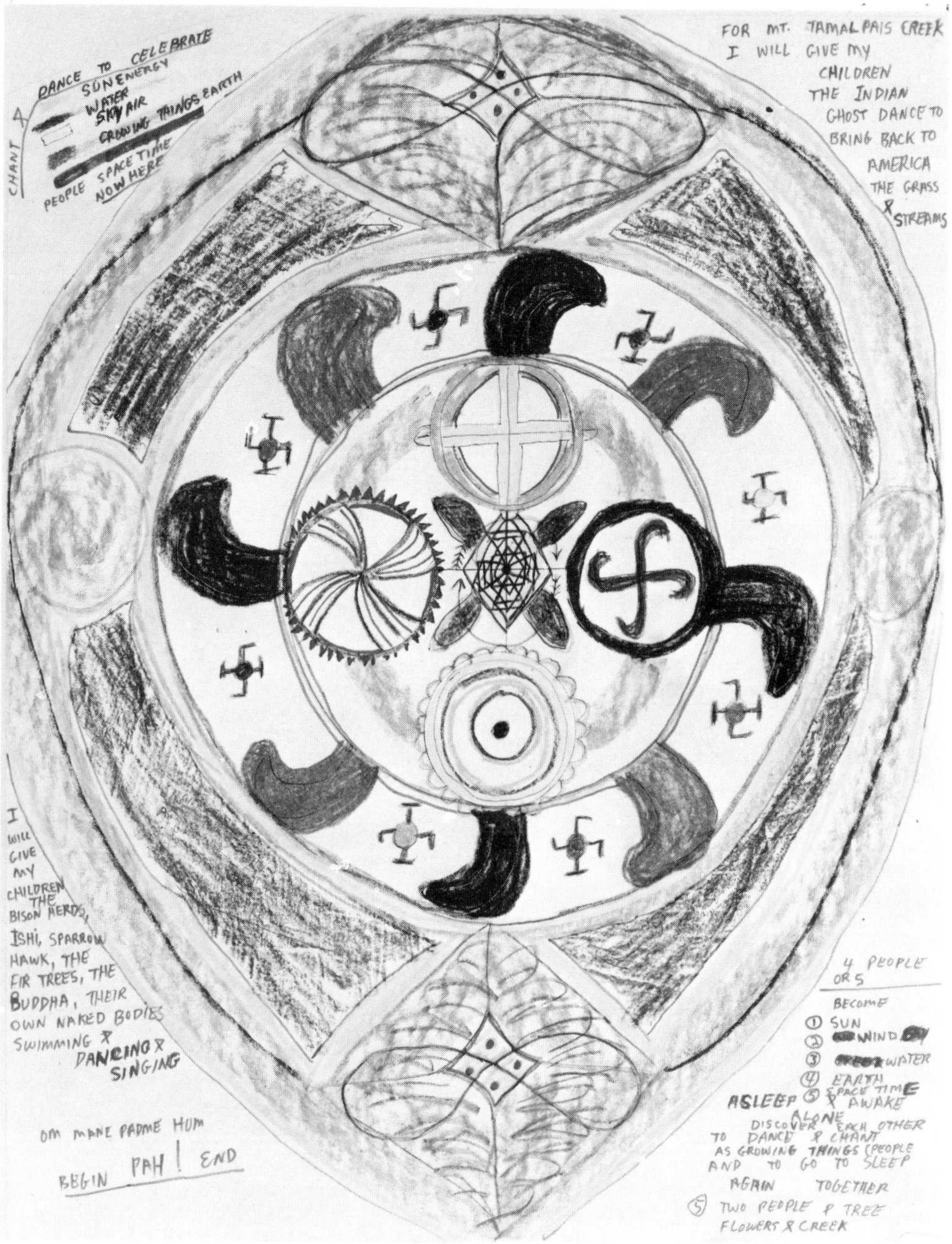

DANCE TO CELEBRATE
SUN ENERGY
WATER
SKY AIR
GROWING THINGS EARTH
PEOPLE SPACE TIME
NOW HERE
CHANT
FOR MT. TAMALPAIS CREEK
I WILL GIVE MY
CHILDREN
THE INDIAN
GHOST DANCE TO
BRING BACK TO
AMERICA
THE GRASS
& STREAMS
I
WILL
GIVE
MY
CHILDREN
THE
BISON HERDS,
ISHI, SPARROW
HAWK, THE
FIR TREES, THE
BUDDHA, THEIR
OWN NAKED BODIES
SWIMMING &
DANCING &
SINGING
OM MANE PADME HUM
BEGIN PAH! END
4 PEOPLE
OR 5
BECOME
① SUN
② WIND
③ WATER
④ EARTH
⑤ SPACE TIME
ASLEEP & AWAKE
ALONE
DISCOVER EACH OTHER
TO DANCE & CHANT
AS GROWING THINGS (PEOPLE
AND TO GO TO SLEEP
AGAIN TOGETHER
⑤ TWO PEOPLE & TREE
FLOWERS & CREEK

A chant and dance score by Woody Nance, performed by a group of Marin County teenagers to protest the destruction of Tamalpais Creek. Tam Creek was a lovely tree-lined meandering stream enjoyed by all the children in the neighborhood. The Army Corps of Engineers, against the residents' desires, cut down the trees and converted the creek to a concrete-lined ditch. Many "establishment types" stood knee deep in the creek with their children as a last stand when all other means failed, which resulted in mass arrests. This dance and sing was composed by members of the Halprin composition class as an invocation to the spirit gods of the creek. Symbols suggest floor patterns and performers started from the center and radiated out to become one in spirit with the cosmic universe. The author has a special relation to this dance since he and his daughter, Rana, were both hauled, forcibly, from the creek and arrested for attempting to stop the desecration.

Within a delicately balanced ecosystem the precise results of a variation of input by individuals or groups, by new inputs or the change of others cannot be completely forecast. The score must remain open. What the score *can* do is "show" the new input and disclose that, obviously, it will make an ecological input and the score will be changed. The Valuaction (V) may also come too late to change the input and therefore the score is doubly important because it can reveal ecological effects before they occur, allowing for selective feedback and decision-making.

There have been very dramatic examples of ecosystems which have been adversely affected by the introduction of one "new" element into the system without any appreciation of how this would affect the score. The classic example is the rabbit in Australia which was introduced as an easy source of food and pelts more than a hundred years ago. Results were disastrous. Since the normal ecological controls were nonexistent, the rabbit spread like wildfire, devastating the countryside at the rate of about seventy square miles per year. The rabbits—foraging for food—ate everything in sight, except the largest trees, and created a virtual desert which became a serious threat to the sheep and cattle grazing industry—the mainstay of the country's economy.

Another example is the mongoose in the Virgin Islands, introduced to control the snakes which it did, indeed, do. It also has effectively destroyed all the eggs of ground-nesting birds in the Islands to the extent that these have become virtually extinct. Often ecosystems can be altered adversely—changed so they no longer exist as climax organisms—by too much human intervention in the form of tender-loving care. By control of burning in the prairies of the Middle West, for example, men have altered their ecology to such an extent that the original ecosystem exists now in very few places (one is being reconstituted at the University of Wisconsin by purposely setting fire to a small museumlike prairie area "on campus"). The floor of the valley at Yosemite National Park, which for centuries was open meadow within which fires burned out seedling trees, has been altered, within the memory of man, by prevention of fires, until now the meadows are becoming forested. This is not necessarily an adverse effect but it *is* occurring due to the conscious intervention of man, and many people are concerned because it is effectively changing the "look and feel" of the valley. The great virtue of ecological scoring is as much to make processes visible and understandable as to control them. One can then work with the new scoring elements in anticipating change and the consequences of affirmative action rather than being caught by surprise. Chance inputs in ecological scoring have their great dangers, as long as we wish to make human-oriented evaluations of what happens. Witness the offshore oil drilling at Santa Barbara.

One of the major factors in ecological scoring is, in fact, the impact of man within an ecosystem. Man has for centuries reacted on ecosystems; it is fallacious to believe that he has not. Man himself *is* part of the ecology of regions. In fact, vast areas of the North American continent have ecological configurations markedly influenced by primitive man. Burning, hunting, clearing underbrush, have been practiced by the Indians for centuries. What emerged was a balanced community of human + nature in which the relationship was intricate and functionally symbiotic. It also became philosophically symbiotic. Indians saw themselves as part of nature. They did not control it, they existed within it. To them, what we now call ecology formed the very basis of their existence.

Even language has ecological and cultural implications. It is well known, for example, that Western culture has produced languages which are extremely limited in describing natural events or nature itself. For other cultures more deeply involved with nature, language is much more descriptive of the subtleties of the man-nature relationship. For example, Eskimos who live constantly with snow have developed words descriptive of varying snow conditions: "falling snow, snow on the ground, snow packed hard like ice, slushy snow, wind-driven flying snow"—we have one word for snow (from *Nonverbal Communication,* Jurgen Ruesch, Weldon Kees). On the other hand, we who are urban-oriented have many words to describe streets: boulevard, street, arterial, alley, lane, freeway, expressway, parkway, avenue. This is perhaps symbolic of our differences.

Primitive man did not pull apart from or lord it over nature; he simply was an element within it. Each affected the other and reacted to the interrelatedness. This is not dissimilar from the Oriental vision of man as part of nature. The *I Ching* score, as I pointed out earlier, is not thought to be really a matter of chance. If man *is* part of nature and the universe, then everything he does influences everything else and is influenced in turn by it. If you lean to the right the whole world tilts in that direction, if only slightly. Thus, the *I Ching* simply adapts to this interrelatedness and is an echo of it. So also for Indians and other primitive people—they did not control nature, they were part of it. It is a concept difficult for Westerners to comprehend; we have always assumed nature on the one hand and ourselves outside of it. Nature for us is a base of man's operation, not man as part of nature's operation. Even when we appreciate nature we are outside looking in, "enjoying" it or using it for food or recreation or economic gain.

Part of the implication of this attitude is that we tend always to see the effects of processes on nature in the way it affects us. For example, fire in a forest we consider bad because it decimates timberlands; earthquakes are bad because they destroy our possessions; even a marsh may be "bad" because the land breeds mosquitoes and cannot be "used." The desert is bad because it does not fit our image of a place to live, which should be "green." Thus we control fire; build on earthquake faults but "try" to engineer our structures so they will survive; fill the marshes needlessly; and plant grass in desert areas where water is scarce. And so on.

Every reader can add endlessly to this list. This anthropomorphic view of ecological processes can be not only myopic, as these examples demonstrate, but also very limited when taken out of context.

The worst of it is that we do not perceive our part of nature as in any way related to all other parts, and we reject the implications of this kind of ecological antiethic. There is perhaps (we say), no hurt in cutting down a few trees in our own neighborhood or on our own property—after all we "own" them and we have the "right" to our own property. Or of grading off an entire hill in order to fill a valley so that tract houses can be built, particularly if "we" are a developer and have bought the hill as a cheap source of "fill" land. Or, of filling in a marsh to build a factory or houses. Even though each one of these has completely altered—perhaps completely destroyed—a valuable ecological unit, perhaps it is viewed as too small for us to worry about too much, and in each case the sacred "ethic" of private property is at stake. Then, however, the effects start snowballing. The lessons from the score have not been noted or cared for. And the inevitability of the course of change starts to affect all of us. What started as a series of private matters soon become community matters. Because trees are cut down the forest floor and its mulches are lost. Then, when winter rains come and pour down the slopes they gouge the hillsides and cause slides. Hilltops have been graded and the valleys filled. On the denuded slopes the houses start to slide, and in the valleys mudslides ooze through the front of the factory and out the back. Down in the marsh not only has the heron long been gone and the fish-spawning places destroyed, but then the floods come and inundate the valley. Lacking any catchment basin to hold them or any backup places for high tides from the estuaries to rise safely into, the factories and houses flood—some wash away. To prevent this, the river for miles upstream has to be put into a concrete ditch to try to carry the water away, the hilltop houses require retaining walls and increased protection, the ravaged hills must be regraded and seeded to slow down the water erosion, but the cycle of destruction and uglification continues, unending. The process of recovery to some stable ecological balance will take centuries—until perhaps, the houses are gone, the silt washed away, the concrete ditches destroyed, no equable balance will be established because the message of the score was ignored and no attempt was made to work within the ecological process.

Because as a society we do not intend specific accidental deaths and have no knowledge of them in their specificity, we feel that no moral issue is involved; yet we adopt social patterns whose inexorable consequence is death to tens of thousands.

Abraham Kaplan, *Life or Death: Ethics and Options*

Often the implications of actions are not clear and that is why mistakes are made. Often it is sheer ignorance of the ecological process that is at issue, the lack of understanding that we *are* part of nature and that we violate her balances at our own risk. I fear that *most* often the reason is that developers do not care a damn for the implications of their actions, so long as they return profit on their investment. As an aside, I feel that we are all responsible for seeing to it that this "motivation" is unacceptable to society.

Technological man has a greater ecological responsibility than pre-technological man in this regard. Primitive man operated slowly—often by trial and error in small increments. Each step in the process could be observed, failures noted and rectified on a small scale. Now the consequences of the massive insults and intrusions of technological man are enormous and far reaching. A freeway can be built through a river valley in a matter of months, moving millions of cubic yards of earth and thousands of people, and changing the ecological balance and aesthetic and social values of a whole region. When that is done the effects are too late to rectify, or modify, or alter. That is why we, more than ever before, need to score our work carefully according to ecological principles. We need to learn to "read" the individual scores inherent in nature and then develop a "master score" which incorporates all of these and develops an agreed upon and positive line of action for the on-going process.

Yet, these typical disasters are comparatively minor compared to what lies ahead of mankind, on a global basis, unless we take immediate ecological action. There is, indeed, increasing evidence that unless we take the *ecological view* and act quickly upon it our planet as an environment for humans to live in will be destroyed within a very few decades. What started as a matter of enlightened self-interest has

increasingly become a matter of sheer survival. More and more, evidence piles up from responsible scientists everywhere that we are running out of time and that we face, in the very near future, what Dr. Paul Ehrlich has called an "eco-catastrophe," an environmental collapse. This eco-catastrophe will very conceivably destroy most of this planet's population unless we take immediate and positive action to stop the use of pesticides, husband the use of our resources, stop air and water pollution immediately, and limit our exploding global population.
Men must learn once again how to live in nature without destroying her balances, as well as to preserve her intact. We must, as well, learn to share our wealth, live as families, begin really to educate our young, and live as a global ecosystem. We have plenty of facts to deal with—it is our interpretation which is yet over-simple. It is not ecology but our understanding of it that is imprecise. *It is ourselves who lack four-dimensional eyesight, not ecology which lacks precision and balance.*

Daniel McKinley, "The New Mythology of 'Man in Nature,'" *The Subversive Science,* Paul Shepard and Daniel McKinley, editors.

Several beginning attempts to plan and build for human occupation have been made, based as much as possible on an understanding of the consequences of action on the ecology of areas. One that I have worked on personally, which exemplifies this idea and the principle of ecological scoring, is the Sea Ranch, which started in 1962 and whose Performance (P) it is now already possible to analyze (V).

NOTHING FOR THE SAKE OF THE EARTH

Everything has been fucked over/the planet is a pig sty...because man hates his own body, he defiles the earth...religion tells him to deny the flesh & a thousand years later he's suprised to discover he's dying...the rape of the environment is almost complete: earth air water & fire have been turned against life/ & we don't even know whether it's possible to save the situation -- or whether the imbalance of the life-system is already so fucked up, that we'll never be able to maintain the conditions necessary for human life...& you can be certain of this, that when nature rejects man & his pollutions, those who remain will be sealed under plastic domes, as unable to walk on the surface of the planet as on the moon/ & it will be just reward for men who paid for their domes by killing off the rest of us...

ecology is yr ass/ if u don't realize it u automatically lose...only those who can conprehend how completely they've fucked things up, can begin to find ways to preserve life, or even approach the solution to the problem of human survival.

ecological information is beginning to appear everywhere, but nobody dares to draw the conclusions/ everyone thinks some little change can be made which will save the situation: stop the cars or stop the population or stop industrial chemical agriculture...very few of us are willing to admit that the ecological situation, taken as a whole, demands the most far reaching changes/ it demands that we destroy every polluting machine & every inorganic cultural form, every social,ethical,political value which interferes with the ecological harmony of man & planet...the ecological situation itself is the most revolutionary fact about our reality/ it is the real crisis which man faces at this historical moment/ & confronted finally with the problem of the destruction of life as a whole, the atomic bomb shrinks down to proportion.

an ecology movement has already begun in california, in response to the growing ecological crisis/ but the movement, so far, has come up with solutions that are worse than the problems: for over-population they end up calling for govt. agencies to control who's fucking & conceiving/ but that amounts to a worse kind of fascism than we have now...what's necessary is new ways of living : the major part of the problem of population will be dealt with when there is a culture in which there are so many other fulfilling things to do that people have fewer children/ & while this isn't the whole solution, it's the principle that must be clear-- we can not impose technology on life without catastrophe/ we must be the ones who learn how to fit technology into a life that is in harmony with the processes of the organic world

there can be no seperation between ecology & politics/ every political act has ecological consequences & every ecological decision is a political demand for control over the use of the resources of the environment... this is no different than the traditional revolutionary problem of controlling the means of production/ but we have carried it further: ecological consciousness transcends economic thinking, because we are forced to consider not just the resources & the machines, but their place in the social structure, their psychological effect on man & their physical effect on the environment...as a science, ecology demands that we integrate all our knowledge & get off our private trips, out of our personal bags, in order to dig what's happening to the planet.

men pollute the earth, but only because they don't imagine nature's anger when they desecrate her body/feeding like a cancer on her surface, sending out their poisons into space/ dumping their shit on the moon... what we see is the technological culture of death, struggling against the natural world/ & nothing short of the truly human, truly sexy, truly communal movement for total liberation, will bring us back to a place where we can begin to live a new life in nature...we are the ones who must build the new culture, changing the whole content of daily life to satisfy our need for total revolution.

nature calls for her lovers to return/ we are made from her earth & then given consciousness/ but we forget that it is nature in us, transmuting herself from matter into knowing/ it is nature moving towards the cosmic consciousness of herself as the whole, total life/ yearning to fill the galaxies with conscious, sensual beings.

earth/life defense

The Sea Ranch, a ten-mile-long development, on the coast of California one hundred miles north of San Francisco, was planned and development started in 1962. It was, right from the beginning, agreed that ecological scoring (S) would play a major role in the decision-making process (V) and that the planning of the coast would be largely based on ecologically sound criteria. We approached it with enthusiasm, feeling that this area could be a prototype of how man could plan development *with* nature rather than ignore her!

A year of careful ecological studies revealed a great deal about the land which was not apparent at the start. It was found by precise meteorological and wind studies along the shore that the wind which is strong could be controlled by particular types of architectural design—by slopes on roofs, for example, wind could be funneled up and over protected outdoor living areas, that by locating houses in the lee of existing windrows calm zones ten times the distance of the height of trees could be developed.

Up in the woods forestry practice was studied at length and a careful logging program was developed which thinned out weak trees, developed views and allowed sunlight into the forest floor. And a carefully organized program of controlled burns removed accumulated litter from the forest floor, overcame the danger of hot disastrous fire, and fertilized the valuable choked out understory of ferns and rhododendron.

Along the coastline the

entire sea front has been left open by organizing housing into tight villagelike clusters of houses and apartments so that each has its views—everyone has access to the coast and no wall of obstructive buildings fences in what has been left for everyone to enjoy. Common areas of green envelop the buildings and form a matrix for living.

Buildings are of wood and shingle—roofs follow the pitch and slope of the hills—seemingly grow out of the land on which they are built. The architecture and the land enhance each other and what has been planned is an environment in which man and nature, with mutual respect, look after each other in a biologically ordered way.

The Sea Ranch
environment—redwood-forested
uplands, meadowed ocean terraces,
rocky cliffs, sandy beaches, and a
very active ocean.

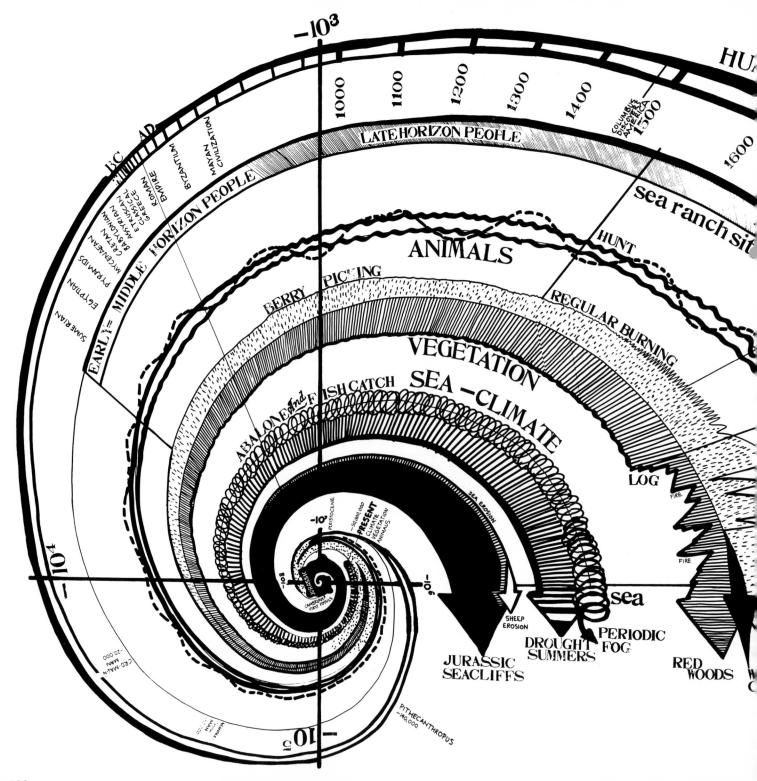

SEA RANCH ECOSCORE

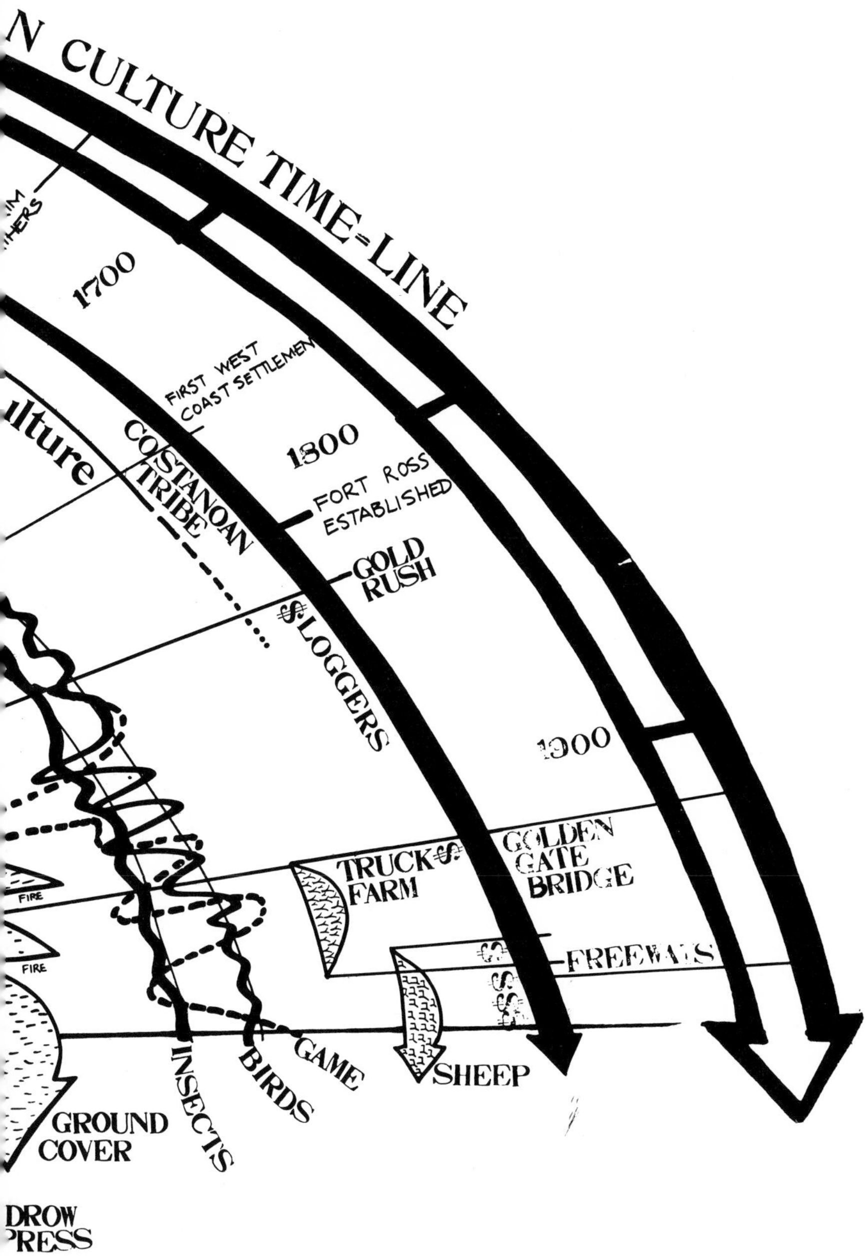

N CULTURE TIME-LINE

1700

FIRST WEST
COAST SETTLEMEN

1800

FORT ROSS
ESTABLISHED

GOLD
RUSH

lture

COSTANOAN
TRIBE

LOGGERS

1900

TRUCK
FARM

GOLDEN
GATE
BRIDGE

FREEWAYS

SHEEP

GAME

BIRDS

INSECTS

FIRE

FIRE

GROUND
COVER

DROW
PRESS

Ecoscore, illustrating the impact of man on the land at Sea Ranch in a geological perspective. The history of the earth begins 2000M years ago at the center of the spiral the primary geological evidence dates from the Cretaceous (60–130M years ago or before -10^6 on the logarithmic scale) and is visible in the coarse conglomerates, sandstones, and shales of the seacliff. It is not until six-thousand years ago that aboriginal man first put his imprint on the land and only one hundred years ago since western man first cut the redwoods here. On the logarithmic time scale, therefore, man's total occupancy in point of actual years at Sea Ranch is insignificant. Yet the broad base of the spiral (at the year 1962 when development began at Sea Ranch) represents man's present enormous potential power to control and to create. These opportunities are considered later under Valuaction (V) and Performance (P). Under ecoscore, man's impact is not evaluated, simply noted as an existential fact of the score.

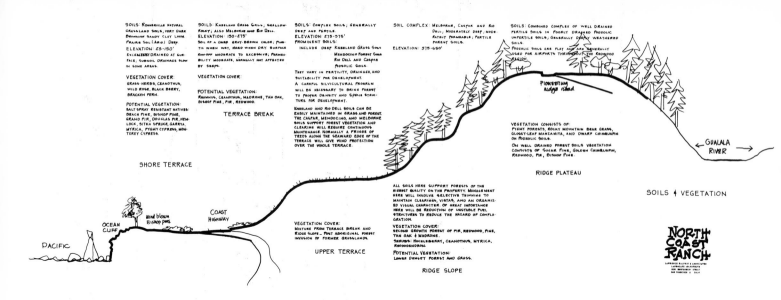

The ecoscore for Sea Ranch—this same scoring figure may be used for any definable area under study—plots the processes by which the Sea Ranch became what it was in 1962 (at the start of planning). In earliest times (beginning of the spiral) these processes include only natural forces, such as geological forces, climatic periods, vegetation, and so forth. The spiral continues into the Quaternary (recent) when pioneer human activities begin to operate and are scored, such as the Indians who hunted and burned but had a light impact on the land, followed by loggers and sheepherders with more massive impact, and now into the present use of the Sea Ranch as a second home community.

In terms of geological time man's total occupancy of Sea Ranch is insignificant, yet his actual and continuing influence is not. The place very much carries the imprint of cultural practices (the meadows,

124

windrows, erosion), and from 1962 the development itself. It is of major concern here that this continuing impact will not divest the place of its uniqueness; that man's part in the ecology be a constructive one.

The ecoscore is a description of processes leading to the inventory items (R) analyzed as the basis for planning. It should, of course, be made clear that an ecoscore does not stop at a particular point in time, but is continuously evolving.

Following the development of the ecoscore, the Sea Ranch was planned and is shown here according to the RSVP cycles.

Resources (R). Resources were carefully catalogued, the physical inventory developed, aesthetic qualities and recreational values analyzed and listed, and "objectives and motivations" enunciated.

"Thematic" Scores. Resource analysis was followed by "thematic" early scores (S) which meant taking particular elements and scoring alternatives as test runs to disclose options and allow for valuaction and selectivity to operate.

Valuaction (V). Valuaction followed hard on the heels of "thematic" scores and made selections between various alternatives based on values and congruence with motivations. Feedback between V and thematic scores was continuous during this period.

Community Scores (S). A final set of scores was then developed as a result of R and V and based on early thematic scores. One was a locational score, another was action-oriented, and the community score also included detailed scores which progress from general principles to very specific "guidelines for action" and specific plans.

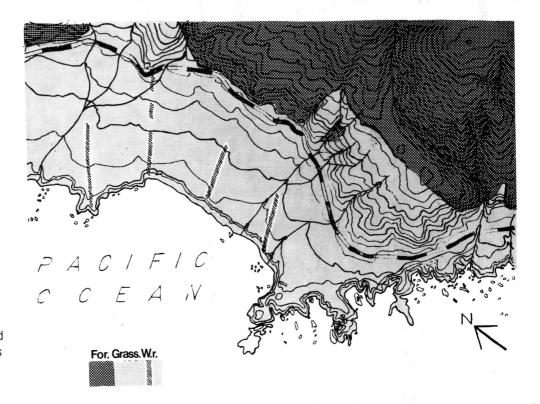

Vegetation. Dark tone indicates upland forest community. Light tone indicates terrace grassland on which windrows occur (indicated by hatching).

For. Grass. W.r.

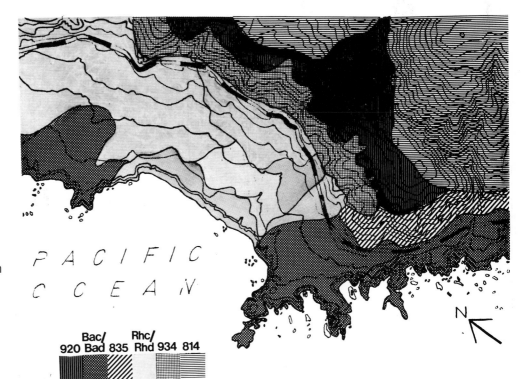

Soils. This map is a source from which the following information was derived:
Depth and natural fertility
Erosion hazard
Permeability and available water capacity
Soil texture
Suitabilities and recommended uses

Bac/ 920 Bad 835 Rhc/ Rhd 934 814

125

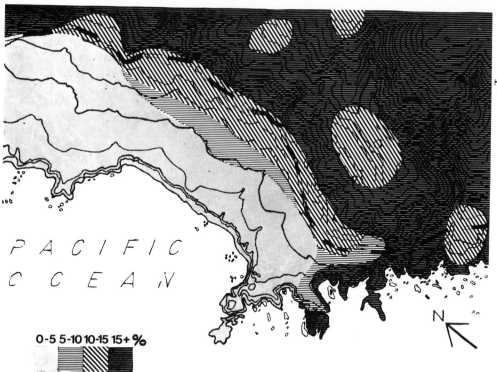

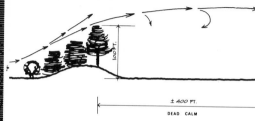

PACIFIC OCEAN

0-5 5-10 10-15 15+ %

N

PACIFIC OCEAN

Perennial streams | Indeterminate drainage | Poorly drained soils

N

Slopes. Lightest tones are areas below 5 per cent; darkest those above 15 per cent.

Surface Drainage. Solid lines are perennial streams. Broken line indicates indeterminate drainage. Tone indicates poorly drained soils.

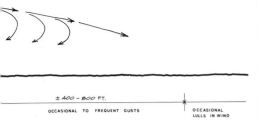

± 400 - 800 FT.

OCCASIONAL TO FREQUENT GUSTS

OCCASIONAL
LULLS IN WIND

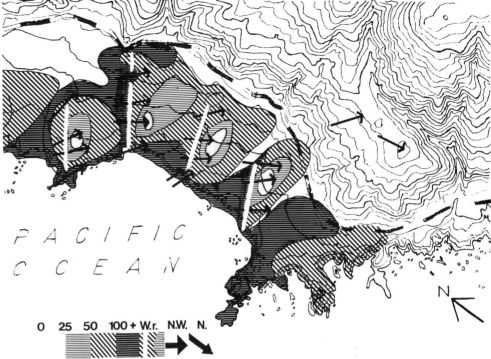

PACIFIC OCEAN

0 25 50 100 + W.r. N.W. N.

Wind Deflection. Lighter tones indicate reduction of wind speeds behind the windrows as a percentage of the maximum speed (darkest tone). Prevalent winds from the north; strongest winds are from the northwest.

Wind Deflection. Wind speeds expressed as a percentage of the maximum speed at the source (indicated by arrow). The lightest tone immediately behind the windrow indicates a 75 per cent reduction in wind speed.

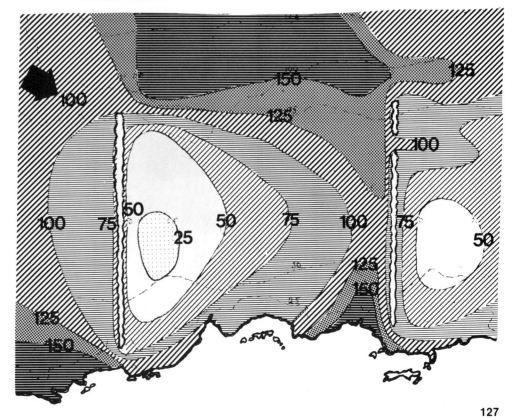

127

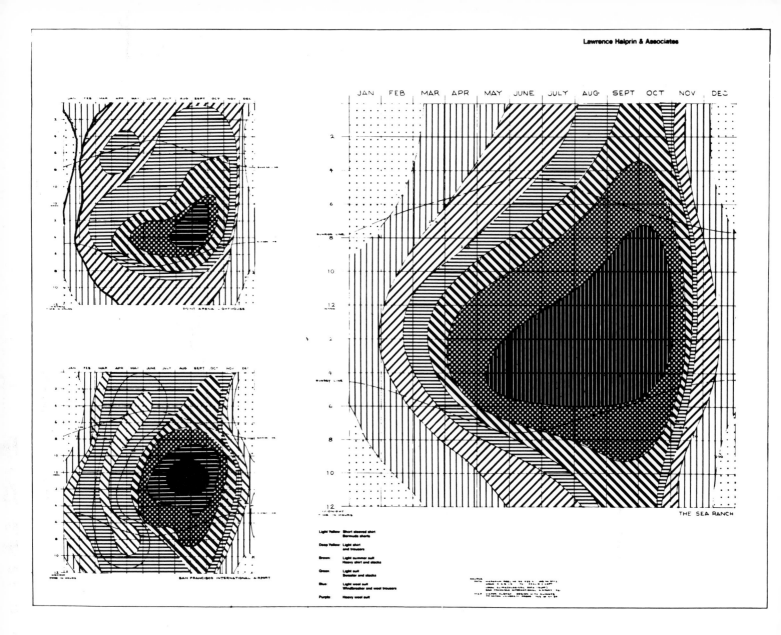

Table of Bioclimatic Needs. Dark tones indicate time of day and year when human radiant heat demands are lowest, *i.e.,* below fifty BTU's per hour per square foot. Lightest tones indicate need for light overcoat.

128

Radiation Impact Chart. Amount of solar energy in BTU's per square foot per hour falling on 45° surface for each cardinal direction throughout the year.

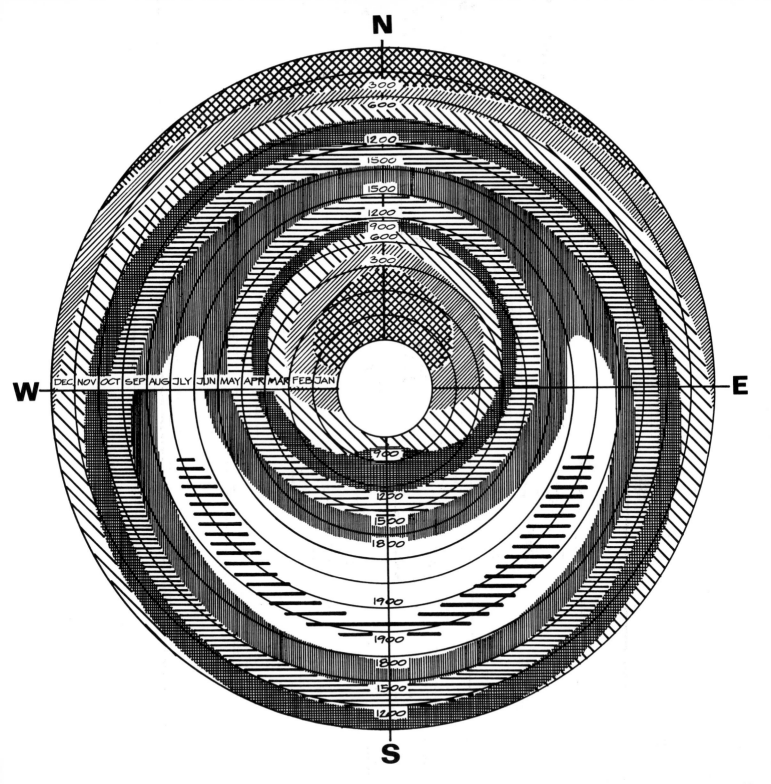

N

W DEC NOV OCT SEP AUG JLY JUN MAY APR MAR FEB JAN E

S

300
600
1200
1500
1500
1200
900
600
300
900
1200
1500
1800
1900
1900
1800
1500
1200

129

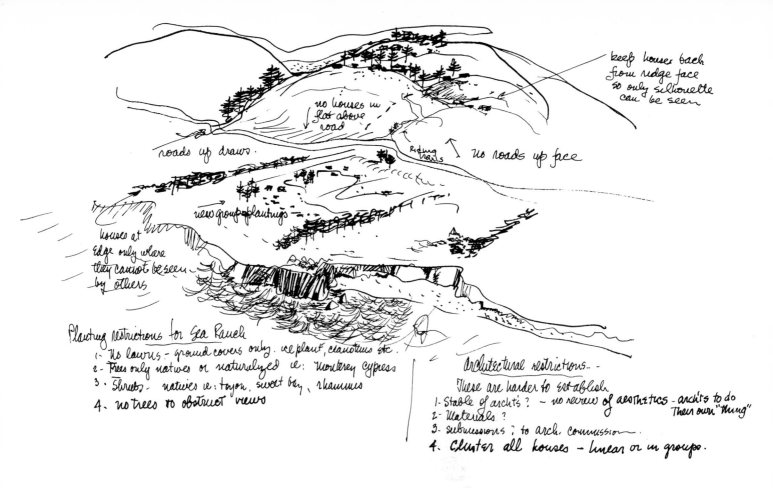

keep houses back
from ridge face
so only silhouette
can be seen

no houses in
flat above
road

roads up draws.

Riding trails   ↑ no roads up face

new group plantings

houses at
edge only where
they cannot be seen
by others

Planting restrictions for Sea Ranch
1- No lawns - ground covers only. ice plant, ceanothus etc.
2- Trees only natives or naturalized ie: Monterey Cypress
3- Shrubs - natives ie: toyon, sweet bay, rhamnus
4- no trees to obstruct views

Architectural restrictions - -
These are harder to establish
1- Stable of arch'ts? - no review of aesthetics - arch'ts to do
2- Materials?   Their own "thing"
3- submissions; to arch. commission.
4- Cluster all houses - linear or in groups.

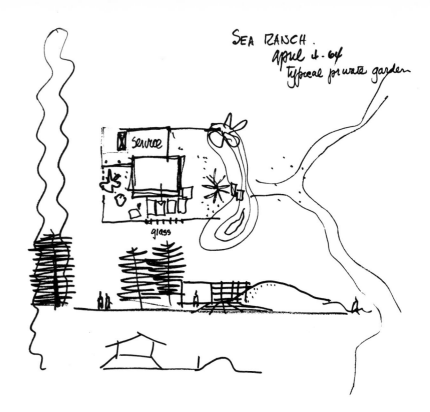

SEA RANCH.
April 4 · 64
typical private garden

service

glass

Sea Ranch – apr 4-64
Scheme for lot alignment along
the cypress windrows at rt 45
to the beach – Linear cluster

These are typical "thematic" early
scores to test out ideas and make
them explicit. From these and others
a group of themes was developed
which were joined together to make
up the final community score.

131

Concept Alternatives

valuation

	Esthetics	Functional	Sociological	Ecological	Long range cost	Short range cost
Utilize & reinforce natural drainage systems						
Construct Systems						
Cut/fill operations respecting natural system						
Ignoring it						
Soil stabilization by seeding						
No stabilization						
Windrow renewal planting						
No renewal planting						
Fencing and grazing meadows						
No management controls						
Clearing and prescribed burning						
No management controls						
Clustered housing						
Scattered housing						
Single family						
Condominium						
Open space pooled as commons						
Open space divided as private lots						
Roads up face						
Roads up draws						
Houses on flat above road						
Houses not on flat above road						
Houses at cliffs edge						
Houses back from cliffs edge						
Houses in forest						
Houses in front of tree line						
Houses behind windrows						
Houses in meadows						
Vary income level						
Maintain single income level						
Slope roofs						
Flat roofs						
Natural materials						
Exotic materials						
Lawns						
Enclosed gardens						
Encourage mixture of uses						
Residential only						

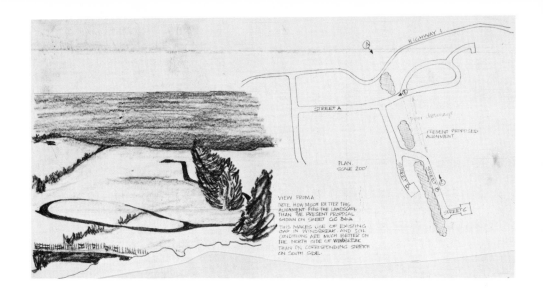

VIEW FROM A
NOTE HOW MUCH BETTER THIS
ALIGNMENT FITS THE LANDSCAPE
THAN THE PRESENT PROPOSAL
SHOWN ON SHEET GC 36a
THIS MAKES USE OF EXISTING
GAP IN WINDBREAK AND SOIL
CONDITIONS ARE MUCH BETTER ON
THE NORTH SIDE OF WINDBREAK
THAN ON CORRESPONDING STRETCH
ON SOUTH SIDE.

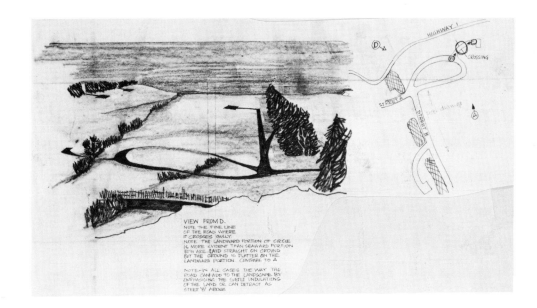

VIEW FROM D.
NOTE THE FINE LINE
OF THE ROAD WHERE
IT CROSSES GULLY
NOTE THE LANDWARD PORTION OF CIRCLE
IS MORE EVIDENT THAN SEAWARD PORTION
BOTH ARE LAID STRAIGHT ON GROUND
BUT THE GROUND IS FLATTER ON THE
LANDWARD PORTION. CONTRARY TO A

NOTE—IN ALL CASES THE WAY THE
ROAD CAN ADD TO THE LANDSCAPE BY
EMPHASISING THE GENTLE UNDULATIONS
OF THE LAND OR CAN DETRACT AS
STREET 'B' ABOVE.

**Thematic scores developed through
concept alternatives in which
alternate futures are tested by
Valuaction decisions.**

**Alternative scores shown graphically
by perspective drawings of roads
either "going with" the land form or
imposed on it.**

Alternative score contrasting typical
sharp engineered cut for road with
the proposal for a Sea Ranch road
that is "rolled into" the land form.

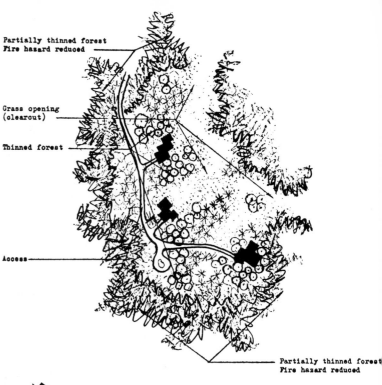

Partially thinned forest
Fire hazard reduced

Grass opening
(clearout)

Thinned forest

Access

Partially thinned forest
Fire hazard reduced

Approx. scale: 1" = 200'

Redwood-pine forests on upland ridges had been logged eighty to ninety years previously and much second growth was weak and diseased and litter on the forest floor was choking out underbrush. Controlled thinning and burns were carried on for a year before development started. This strengthened remaining trees, opened up views, allowed light into the forest which rejuvenated the understory of fern and rhododendron.

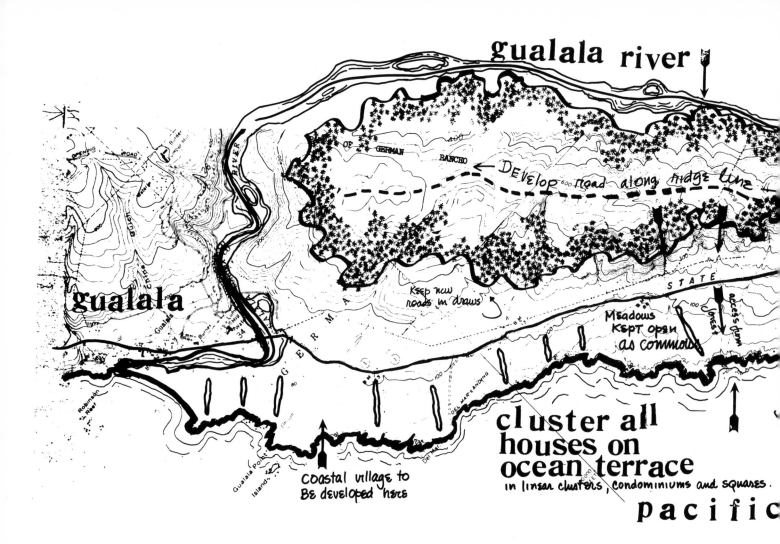

gualala river

OF GERMAN RANCHO

← DEVELOP road along ridge line

gualala

Keep new roads in draws

Meadows KEPT open as commons

access from

STATE

Coastal village to Be developed here

cluster all houses on ocean terrace
in linear clusters, condominiums and squares.

pacific

The locational "score" for the Sea Ranch establishes major land policies and where they are to occur on the land. Following inventories of Resource (R) we tried many "thematic," *i.e.,* partial scores, to test our alternatives. Many of these are indicated on the Valuaction chart. Some examples are: housing in clusters or housing scattered, houses along coast or kept away from coast, etc. These thematic scores were then tested out to see what the consequences of each action would be; for example, if houses were lined up along the coast only those living in the houses would have beach access and

the visual quality of the area would be destroyed. After testing the "themes" Valuactions (V) were made and the master scorer made his selections, for example, "all houses need to be clustered." These selections formed the basis for the master score which establishes major "lines of action" for performers to follow. It sets forward the "what and why" of future action and allows the "how" of performance to emerge from the creative input of future architects and planners when working on specific detailed projects following the master score.

SEA RANCH

Lawrence Halprin & Associates

·5000 ACRES·

☞ LOCATIONAL SCORE

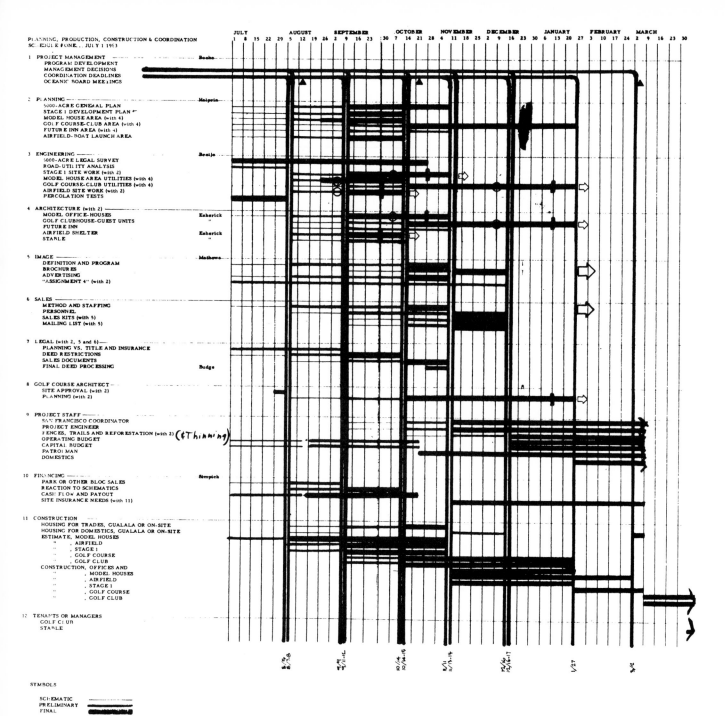

SEA RANCH
july '63

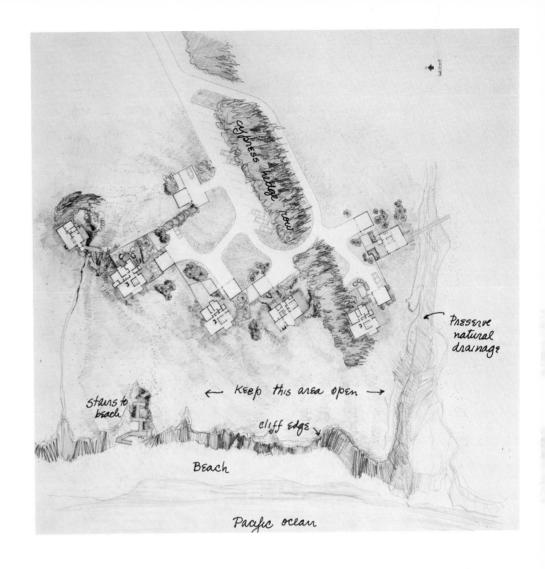

Within the sketch:
cypress hedge row

Preserve natural drainage

← Keep this area open →

Stairs to beach

cliff edge ↓

Beach

Pacific ocean

Score for the planning and early construction process—a chart developed by the owners for the first year of planning. Al Boeke, Director of Planning for Oceanic Properties.

The first "cluster" of houses designed around a hedgerow and linking all houses into a villagelike quality. Each house has a protected garden, roof lines control wind and follow the line of the cypress hedge. Ocean front left completely open.

Performance (P). **It is now possible to look at and judge performance. Early housing clusters and condominiums lie beautifully in the land, work within an understanding of the major intentions of the score, and make major inputs into the *how* of Performance (P).**

"Cluster" of single family houses around court

Condominium "Cluster" around interior court

House on point -
coastline NOT kept open
Roof line demanding & dominating
"architect-as-hero"

Valuaction (V) of Performance (P).
Unfortunately, later performance has
lost track of the intent of the score
and many performers have not
"gone with" the agreed upon score.
The following photographs show
violations to the master score. It is
significant to analyze why the score
was violated as a guide to future
work in scoring. I have been told
that the score was too open and
should have been more closed and
therefore controlling. I do not agree.
I do not feel that any score is too
open. I feel that I overlooked several

characteristics of scoring,
principally:

1. The score was not visible enough
to everyone involved.

2. Some of the score was kept
secret because it was not completely
agreed upon by management. For
example, public access to beaches
and the idea of varied income. This
did not really turn out to be a
balanced community in terms of
income levels, which it was intended
to be.

3. All the principles of the score
were not understood thoroughly. For
example, the notion of tight-housing
clusters of various configurations
was not really visualized by the sales
force.

4. Early sales management groups
were disbanded, and the second
wave had not been involved in the
score and subsequently did not
really understand it.

5. Short-range economic goals were
allowed to override long-term goals.

146

houses "scattered" not in clusters

houses in front of tree line - on slope which score said "Keep open"

keep houses back from ridge face so only silhouette can be seen

no houses in flat above road

roads up draws

riding trails — no roads up face

new groups of plantings

houses at edge only where they cannot be seen by others

A. GENERAL PLAN OF ORIGINAL SOILS AND GEOLOGY OF MARKET STREET

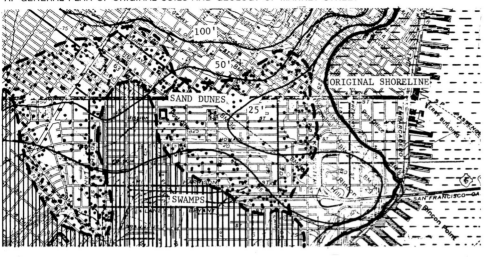

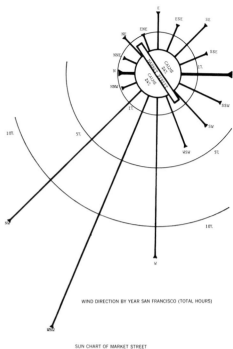

WIND DIRECTION BY YEAR SAN FRANCISCO (TOTAL HOURS)

B. CROSS SECTION OF MARKET STREET

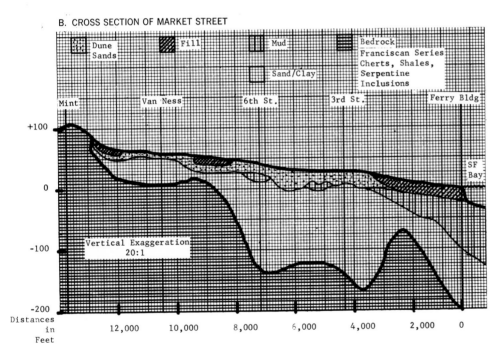

Dune Sands	Fill	Mud	Bedrock Franciscan Series: Cherts, Shales, Serpentine Inclusions
		Sand/Clay	

Mint   Van Ness   6th St.   3rd St.   Ferry Bldg

Vertical Exaggeration 20:1

Distances in Feet: 12,000   10,000   8,000   6,000   4,000   2,000   0

SUN CHART OF MARKET STREET

40° SUN CHART
(40° N. Lat.)

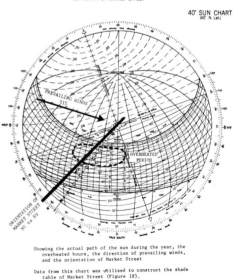

PREVAILING WINDS 51%

ORIENTATION OF MARKET STREET NE to SW

"OVERHEATED" PERIOD

Showing the actual path of the sun during the year, the overheated hours, the direction of prevailing winds, and the orientation of Market Street

Data from this chart was utilized to construct the shade table of Market Street (Figure 18).

Ecological inventories for the redesign of Market Street in San Francisco. These serve as a basis for the ecoscore which has as much significance inside a city as in the natural macrolandscape. Urban living needs to be based on ecoscoring as a basic biological premise of life from which aesthetics derive.

When it gets right down to the core of things, ecological scoring, street scoring, and the new multidimensional urban scoring and all other scoring must be brought together into a new concept of community scoring. In addition to the physical and economic inventory requirements basic to this scoring, there are a host of other elements from the behaviorial sciences, the "social" sciences, and from politics, law, economics, and psychology, which must act as inputs under R in the cycle for such an intricate and elaborate community score to have validity and application. I mean "community" in the ecological sense of the term, namely, "an aggregate of living organisms having mutual relationships among themselves and with their environment." I do not, in my thinking, differentiate as to size or numbers, and certainly not to purpose or motivation. We can have a community when there are three people, and in my view we must shortly come to the realization that all members of this planet Earth are a community. I cannot differentiate philosophically between the needs and urgencies of family planning or village planning or regional planning or urban planning, national planning or international planning—they are all urgent and each has meaning and feedback to the other.

The community score, essentially, is the sum total of all the scoring devices we have been discussing. It scores what amounts to "ecosystems," describing and guiding the processes by which they are to evolve based on all the factors which are required to make them viable. A human community is *in fact* an ecosystem, even though it may have evolved quickly and largely through man-made efforts. The community score needs to have (as an absolutely firm basis) ecoscoring and the disclosures that ecoscoring makes, but it adds many other inputs as well, man-made constructs and requirements such as: transportation, shelter, sewerage, power, and light. It also must inevitably base itself to a considerable measure on economics—the cost of developing the community, the period of amortization and the implementing machinery required to achieve it. Finally, the community score will go beyond ecoscoring into areas of Valuaction (V); cultural patterns which are themselves distillations of values and selectivity, and the aesthetic implications of the communities' structure: what the score's impact will be on the lifestyle of its inhabitants. Ecoscoring by and in itself cannot have a value system since it produces its own values which inevitably are nonjudgmental and purely process-oriented. It is not that value selectivity (V) cannot be applied to the importance of ecological "decisions." These can and need to come under the valuaction portion of our idealized procedural system. But the scoring of ecosystems itself is nonjudgmental; we have seen before, that natural processes themselves have no built-in values. They have no program or purpose (or motivation unless you consider a food chain or an energy cycle a motivation); they themselves as processes *are* their own purpose, constitute their own value and their own reason for being. Ecology *is* value. For example, a growing tree does not have to demonstrate its purpose. It simply *is*.

This kind of ecological "value" is similar to the Jungian notion of "individuation," that is, the process by which a man lives out his innate human nature. Jung wrote: "People living in cultures more securely rooted than our own have less trouble in understanding that it is necessary to give up the utilitarian attitude of conscious planning in order to make way for the inner growth of the personality."

There is a wonderful Chinese story (related by Chuang Tzu) that bears on this notion of existential value in nature exemplified by the tree.

A wandering carpenter, called Stone, saw on his travels a gigantic old oak tree standing in a field near an earth-altar. The carpenter said to his apprentice, who was admiring the oak: "This is a useless tree. If you wanted to make a ship, it would soon rot; if you wanted to make tools, they would break. You can't do anything useful with this tree, and that's why it has become so old."

But in an inn, that same evening, when the carpenter went to sleep, the old oak tree appeared to him in his dream and said: "Why do you compare me to your cultivated trees such as whitethorn, pear, orange, and apple trees, and all the others that bear fruit? Even before they can ripen their fruit, people attack and violate them. Their branches are broken, their twigs are torn. Their own gifts bring harm to them, and they cannot live out their natural span. That is what happens everywhere, and that is why I have long since tried to become completely useless. You poor mortal! Imagine if I had been useful in any way, would I have

reached this size? Furthermore, you and I are both creatures, and how can one creature set himself so high as to judge another creature? You useless mortal man, what do you know about useless trees?"

The carpenter woke up and meditated upon his dream, and later, when his apprentice asked him why just this one tree served to protect the earth-altar, he answered, "Keep your mouth shut! Let's hear no more about it! The tree grew here on purpose because anywhere else people would have ill-treated it. If it were not the tree of the earth-altar, it might have been chopped down."

The carpenter obviously understood his dream. He saw that simply to fulfill one's destiny is the greatest human achievement, and that our utilitarian notions have to give way in the face of the demands of our unconscious psyche. If we translate this metaphor into psychological language, the tree symbolizes the process of individuation, giving a lesson to our shortsighted ego.

   Carl G. Jung, **Man and His Symbols**

But community scores *do* deal with values, *are* selective, and *do* imply valuaction. In that sense they are human-oriented and not completely and permissively process-oriented. In the diagram outlining the steps of procedures, community scores will originate with Resources (R), proceed through Score → Performance (S, P), and as part of feedback—involve Valuaction (V): RSVP. There are, there have to be, decisions heavily weighted toward human values placed on the changes and implications of changes brought about by man. Where the slow natural filling in of tarns in the High Sierra has resulted in a shift in the climatic balance and incidentally revealed forms of superb beauty; from bay to filled-up bay is *not* acceptable as a principle in San Francisco Bay. There the community has exercised the Valuaction (V) based on the prognostications from the Score (S), to prevent filling the Bay and thus not allowing it to become a meandering river instead. The accompanying diagram shows San Francisco Bay as it would be if all shallow areas were

BAY or RIVER ?

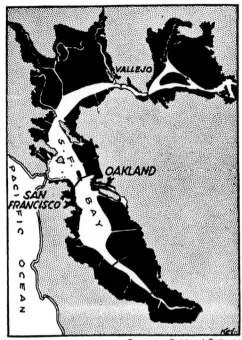

Courtesy Oakland Tribune

The white area, according to an Army Engineer's study, shows what would be left of San Francisco Bay if all shallow parts susceptible of filling were filled.

filled by development. The implications are enormous and wide ranging. The visual character of the Bay would change, but more important the climate, in fact the entire ecology of the region, would be drastically altered. This score dramatizes the urgent need for a valuaction to be made to stop the filling immediately, before irreversible trends are started.

Community scoring is quite different from "trend planning" which is the acceptance of the inevitability of growth per se and then the search for accommodation to inevitability. The ekisticians speak of a global city called "Ecumenopolis," which accepts the notion that all habitable areas on the globe will be filled in and occupied. It is a horrifying thought. Scores can plan for that too, if desirable, but the V section of the RSVP cycles indicates quite clearly that there are possible alternative actions and decisions that are necessary to prevent this kind of global pollution by people. The technologists can plan for anything and even achieve it. The question remains, however, whether that is what is desired by the global community. The greatest eco-disaster we face is the uncontrolled growth of population, and the greatest ally that growth has is the acceptance of this idea as inevitable.

Histories of settlements have not always followed the RSVP cycles and have often moved from pure process through great emphasis on motivation to a point where neither is adequately satisfying our needs. We need to devise new methods for developing communities which have the qualities of inevitability and organic growth that design process alone can bring. But we also now are dealing with much larger populations, intensified speed of planning and building, and a bewilderingly intricate number of technological advances. Programming and its implied motivations also become an essential requirement of our communities. But planning based purely on programming will result in rigidity, formalism, and control. This has been the result in past cities and even today results in many of the same kind of formalistic inadequacies.

Steps in developing a modern community score:

There is much to learn from a review of past communities, how they arose, the processes by which they were built, and their performance. Through an observation of these primitive beginnings we can see vast implications for our more advanced communities; many of the basic lessons are easier to see and more clearly stated.

Early communities which were almost entirely process-oriented tended to grow naturally and had many of the grouping characteristics of groups which result from many individuals in a population aggregated together. As I have pointed out under street scores, the relationship was primarily between units which were not organized along connectors. The pattern therefore tends to be randomized and improvised—performance-oriented, without a score. There is, as inevitably there must be, a relationship between units, just because they aggregate and are "aware" of each other. Each creates enough "personal" space around itself and respects the personal space of others, but remains close enough for a kind of mutual security. Often the distance between units reflects the kind of "living" the organism has to make. If the group is a hunting group the distances must be farther apart than a farming group, or if a population of organisms is large it requires farther distances apart than if it is small.

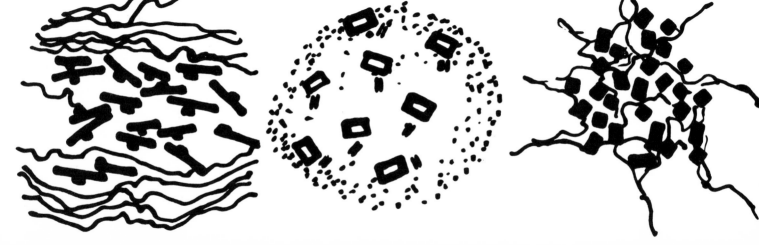

Bedouin tents in the desert near the ancient Nabatean city of Shifteh, Israel.

Hillside settlement, Nepal.

Arabs in desert.

African village.

Le Place de L'Etoile laid out by Baron Haussman, planner to Napoleon III. Formalism rampant within the city based on an axial imagery and internal policing. Any tourist who has ever tried to cross to the Arc de Triomphe through Parisian traffic knows this place as a challenge to pedestrians.

The ideal city developed by Scamozzi based on defense and heavy emphasis on formal organization—A.D. 1615.

Early communities responded in a direct way to the nature of the place they were in. They normally responded strongly to the natural topography, spread out from a center, and the paths and connectors were randomized, based on easiest pedestrian or beast-of-burden routes.

Threshing ground

Arab village outside of Nablus, Israel

mosque

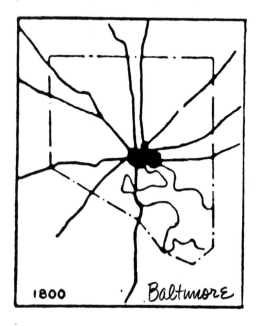

1800 Baltimore

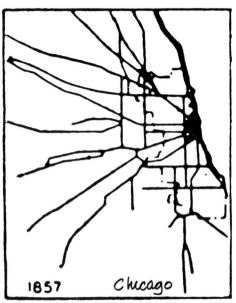

1857 Chicago

If they found themselves constrained to one side, as by the sea or a river, they spread away from it; if it was a hill they spread around.

Often the spreading was done in direct response to very functional needs; if the settlement was in hilly country with stony soil on the hills and rich soil in the valleys, the houses were sited on the hills leaving the valleys for crops. This is typified by Arab villages that live off their own crops in Israel. The preservation of the good valley soil for crops was of course a purely functional (and in that sense an economic) decision.

Today we tend to proceed in the reverse direction and build houses in the flatlands of the valleys and in the process we destroy valuable, irreplaceable crop land. The reasons for this are both economic and technological. With modern mass production of standardized houses, flat land is much cheaper to build upon. On the other hand, with mechanized agriculture based on factory-type warehousing and sales, packaging and transportation, the village close to its fields of rich soil has no more "economic meaning." We may of course find that it has other meanings, regional and philosophic, which should be plugged into the score. These are questions in which short-term economic gain and cost must be weighed against long-term irreversible trends. When rich soil is lost to housing it is forever lost to agriculture. We have been operating for too long on short-term principles without scoring the consequences to the regional and global community.

Early settlements developed almost entirely by process. There was some rudimentary scoring involved, but it was mostly dependent on the physical attributes of the site and the simplest and most urgent requirements for shelter; no elaborate master score was involved or required. The performance came first and by itself. It was essentially an improvisation.

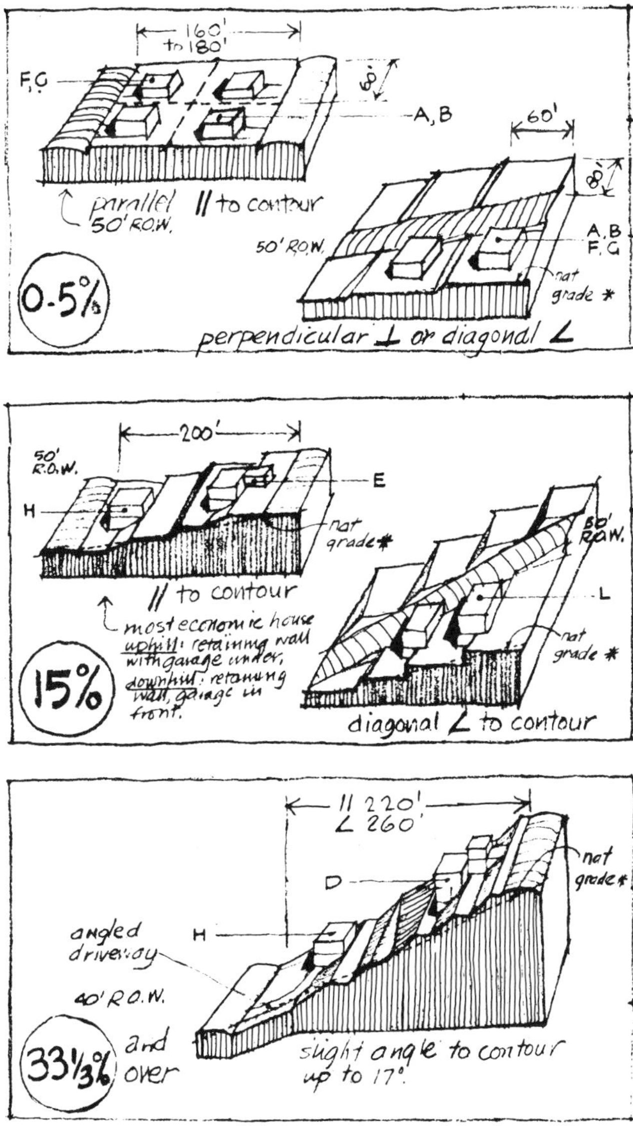

HOUSE SIZE	STREET TYPE	HOUSE TYPE	MINIMUM LOT SIZE
1250	II	A F	60 x 90
1250	⊥≈Z	A F	60 x 90
1600	II	A E F	60 x 90
1600	⊥ or Z	A E F G	60 x 90
2000	II	B G	60 x 90
2000	⊥ or Z	B G	60 x 90

parallel 50' R.O.W. / || to contour / 0-5% / perpendicular ⊥ or diagonal ∠ / nat grade *

HOUSE SIZE	STREET TYPE	HOUSE TYPE	MINIMUM LOT SIZE
1250	II	E H	60 x 80 / 60 x 120
1250	∠	L	45 x 120
1600	II	E H	60 x 80 / 60 x 120
1600	∠	L	45 x 120
2000	II	E H	60 x 80 / 60 x 120
2000	∠	L K	45 x 120 / 60 x 120

|| to contour / most economic house uphill: retaining wall with garage under, downhill: retaining wall, garage in front. / 15% / diagonal ∠ to contour / nat grade *

HOUSE SIZE	STREET TYPE	HOUSE TYPE	MINIMUM LOT SIZE
1250	II	H	80 x 100
1250	II	D	60 x 120
1600	II	H	80 x 100
1600	II	D	60 x 120
2000	II	H	80 x 100
2000	II	D	60 x 120

|| 220' ∠ 260' / nat grade * / angled driveway / 40' R.O.W. / 33⅓% and over / slight angle to contour up to 17°

This series of diagrams is part of an analysis of housing types possible on various slope conditions near San Jose, California. The flatland house normally favored by "developers" can be built for about four thousand to five thousand dollars cheaper than the house-on-slope. As a result the Santa Clara Valley has been converted from a vast productive orchard to a vast sprawling subdivision. Uglification and loss of natural resources has followed short-term profit motives. The alternatives shown in the diagrams on 15 per cent and 33 per cent slopes cost more on a short-term basis but preserve irreplaceable agricultural land.

An example of this kind of performance-oriented (P) community can be easily developed today through experimental "happening-like" events. During several joint environmental workshops, Ann and I have presented simple scores from which communities were built in the same direct and spontaneous way. There were several, very similar factors in the score with resemblances to primitive villages—among them an identity of readily "available" structural materials, in this case driftwood logs.

The first of these "Driftwood Villages" was scored in the simplest and most direct way possible, with minimal

directions to establish the score, and mostly depending on the limitations imposed by the site. The similarities between these workshop communities and actual process-developed ones is very striking. They radiate from centers, they are nonformalistic in form—they are *not* organized strongly around connectors (although they do have connectors which are thinly developed), and the connectors that are there result from the *need* to connect rather than being a major *force* in establishing the form. It is characteristic of more "advanced" communities that they are very strongly based on "connectors," while primitive communities are based on individual units. The other striking

thing which seems to link primitive communities is the very strong equality between individuals and the lack of hierarchical structure in building the community. Perhaps this is *because* they are so process-oriented and not control- or goal-oriented, and also not based on a defined and elaborate program.

The second home community, built on the rubble of the first, has a somewhat stronger score because of its more defined motivation. This second community, perhaps because of its Resource (R) analysis, was more demanding of its builders and required more defined group effort.

Scores for Driftwood villages 1 & 2

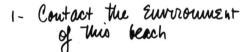

SCORE 1

SCORE (S)	RESOURCES (R)
1- Contact the Environment of this beach 2- Alter the Environment	1- Limiting factors: ~~physical environment~~ 2- 35 People 3- Materials - driftwood, water sand, cliffs wind, seaweed 4- MOTIVATION: According to individual needs & interests.

physical environment (see diagram)

SCORE 2 (S)	RESOURCE (R)
1- Start from the beginning 2- Build a new Environment as a community working together as a group	1- Limiting factor- physical environment of driftwood village 1 2- Same group of people 3- Materials - same 4- MOTIVATION - (a) Giving up old structure is part of the way of finding new ones (b) whatever you do must include your awareness of its impact on the whole group.

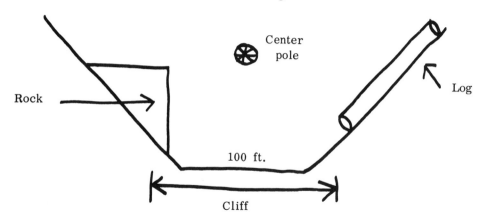

Water's edge

Center pole

Rock →

Log

100 ft.

Cliff

Plan of the Driftwood Village was drawn the day after the event. Each group delineated what it has built separately and in silence and then all groups joined their drawings together. This master score of the event proved to be extremely accurate even though done collaboratively and without discussion or actual measurement.

The reindeers were alarmed by a
helicopter and formed this tight
defensive spiral.

The same is inevitably true in the emerging patterns of real settlements. Soon the most primitive ones were superseded by Resource-oriented ones whose purposes were defined and very clearly postulated, and whose scores, therefore, were more controlling. Programming for communities becomes important the moment they are "threatened"—when pure process is insufficient because it has no goal orientation. This is true not only for physical communities (that is, actual settlements) but also for communities of animals and people. I have observed in workshops that programs have been rejected as freedom-limiting devices, until processes disintegrated into such confusion that the group's survival became threatened. At such a point, even ephemeral groups tend to be forced into the acceptance of the need for Resource as an organizing element so they can proceed clearly into scoring of process. The most common program for early communities was defense, which took several forms; the Roman camp which was a score for a quickly erected striking force and then the walled city.

Later, other programmatic needs (or wishes of the ruling classes) came into play. For instance, monumentality was a very strong motivating force in the design of capital cities. Monumentality remains today a motivating force for the artist-planner as well as for his overweening corporate clients, public or private.

Ideal utopian cities have "goal orientation" as their motivation: the perfection in physical form for which many well-meaning artist-planners have always striven.

Any city which has a strong program which the score serves "to carry out" will have a strong formalistic pattern. The formalism can be symmetrical or asymmetrical—that is not the point. It is the formalism and the rigidity implicit in the formalism that is the issue and is characteristic of this kind of Score-Resource (SR) relationship. Often the motivation (as part of Resource) can be within the master scorer's "image" of what a community form should be like. Though not imposed from outside, it will still develop a formalism of its own. Artists' motivations for themselves in the inner cycle can be as demanding as externally imposed aims. This is part of the artist-as-hero hangup, and the rigidities imposed by artists' preconceptions of results can result in the same kind of preordained and formalized structure. It is the motivation controlling the score which establishes the formalism; when Score (S)—or process—is conceived as a *vehicle,* not an activity with its own results, it causes rigidity to result. Rigidity and sterility are usually synonymous.

The formalized imposed vision of the artist-hero may be acceptable if it is agreed upon by the people and not simply foisted on them. This is particularly true of ephemeral or minor-impact works of art like theatre or atelier painting or sculpture. Then people can choose to relate to or not relate to the work. I can decide not to see a movie or view a work of sculpture or read a book. That is a choice I can make. But in community planning and design or political decision-making I will be forced by the decision of others to accept something that will, in a deep and profound way, affect my lifestyle and my children's for generations. That is why the artist-hero left alone to work out his own struggles for self-realization (in politics or architecture or planning or science or technology) is so dangerous and unacceptable as a basis for community action.

A community of bison regrouping from a scattered configuration to a tight stampede form as a result of threat by Indian hunters.

TARTAR CAMP

FEUDAL EDO

ROMAN FRONTIER TOWN

The preceding page showed crisis impinging on animal communities and forcing them from scattered foraging bands to a tight knot facing outward against the enemy. This instinctive shift in form will, however, change back as soon as the threat is removed. On this page are the same forms taken by human communities for similar defense reasons, these however remain fixed for centuries.

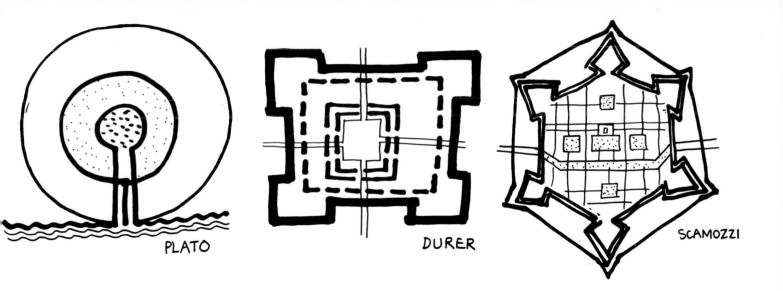

PLATO

DURER

SCAMOZZI

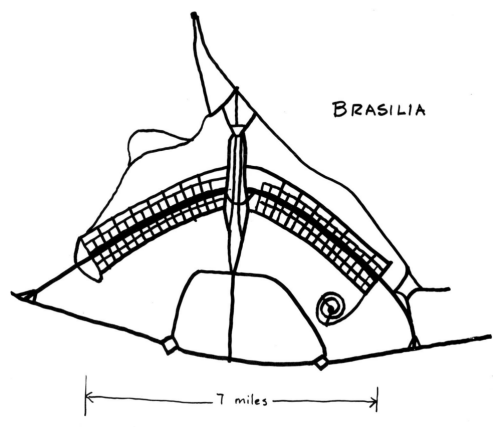

BRASILIA

7 miles

Three utopian ideal city forms—each influenced profoundly the forms of medieval cities. Utopian idealism or any other goal orientation negates process as evolutionary towards structure and instead imposes form.

Brasilia, the new capital of Brazil, was carved out of the jungle and made into a new capital city. It did not evolve and was planned "for the people" who had no participation in the formation of the score. As a result squatters' towns have cropped up all around this monumental new city whose formalism was imposed from outside.

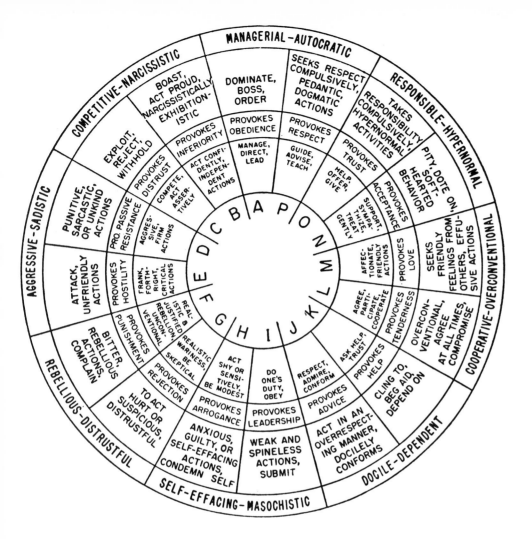

The following names appear in the handwritten diagram:

Paul's homework assignment from Ued

Norma task

Doug   Joe

Dania   Cary

Cibella   Rana   Paul Baum

Paul   Chip   Jim   Paul Baum   alani

Ryan

Suzanne   Rob   Nancy T   Mike   Evelyn   Ted

Rewer   Barbara   Bruce   Rita   Helen   Betty

Eve   Shari   LINDA   Nancy

Norma   Dave   Marilyn   ann   Hanna

Leistiko   Cindy

Dick

Larry   Julie

Chart from early work of Timothy Leary which reveals the causal-resultant interrelation between people based on their own impact on others.

A diagram of a personal interrelationship score within a community of people during a workshop. The spatial positioning of individuals has implied relations to the Gestalt of the group as perceived by the scorer. This configuration was noted down quickly as an assignment and does not relate to physical positioning of the group.

Ephemeral communities or transitory groups of people can exhibit the same kind of dichotomy. If a picnic is planned simply to enjoy eating stuffed eggs and drinking wine, the patterns that emerge from this scoring idea are quite different from when the picnic is planned to honor an event, such as a birthday or a national holiday, or to attain some aim like a "boy-scout outing." The Score (S)—Resource (R) relation operates as well as in ephemeral communities or groups as in permanent ones. As long as a group has no strong motivation from outside related to the outer cycle under (R) it will have no strong pattern or cohesive force because it is made up simply of an aggregate of individuals, or selves, motivated by their own inner cycles. When a group is motivated from outside through pressures of necessity such as defense, or "structures" such as family configurations, or societal ones such as earning a living, the pattern becomes more formalized. This can arise through fear which can become fascistic, or by collective agreement of selves on the basic necessity for configuration to achieve a structure. Perhaps this is a point to remember in the new interest in expanded group living—the new communes. Most of them are extremely well-motivated by aggregates of people seeking self-fulfillment within their own inner cycle. How long this will serve as an organizing principle, however, is unclear. Those centered around specific interests such as theatre, rock groups, special-food restaurant (soul food, organic food, and so forth) operation, are based on both inner and outer cycles. Kibbutz in Israel, of course, has continued partly because of outside threat for three generations.

Scores are required to allow for processes to generate results visibly "before" the Performance (P). Scores make trial and error possible and valuaction and feedback feasible—activities which used to be accomplished slowly during actual process. Scores make it possible for us to explore, to invent, to try configurations for communities before the fact. They enable us to be selective, to understand the consequences of the actions that we will take. This allows us to make significant and long-range decisions in order to build communities in a new technological society where a great deal must be preplanned and prebuilt such as utility systems, road networks, mass transit systems, vast intercommunication networks, and so forth.

A certain order must be developed, of course, to insure equalization of facilities so that one neighborhood will not have all the hospitals and another all the schools. We need to learn from past mistakes; noxious industries producing fumes and noise should be downwind from residential neighborhoods, and children should be able to play away from the constant danger of high-speed vehicles. The RSVP cycles allow this to proceed without closing down on the score as creative process.

It is significant here to differentiate clearly between systems engineering, which is heavily dependent on R in the cycle, and scoring, which is not. In systems engineering the "mission requirements must be determined before establishing the mission," whereas of course in the RSVP cycles requirements develop as part of scoring and in fact emerge from it. Also, systems engineers feel that "social parameters such as health, convenience, aesthetics, and happiness must be quantified before a systems-engineered environment is valid and effective" (W. L. Rogers, "Aerospace Systems Technology and the Creation of Environment," *Environment for Man*, William R. Ewald, editor).

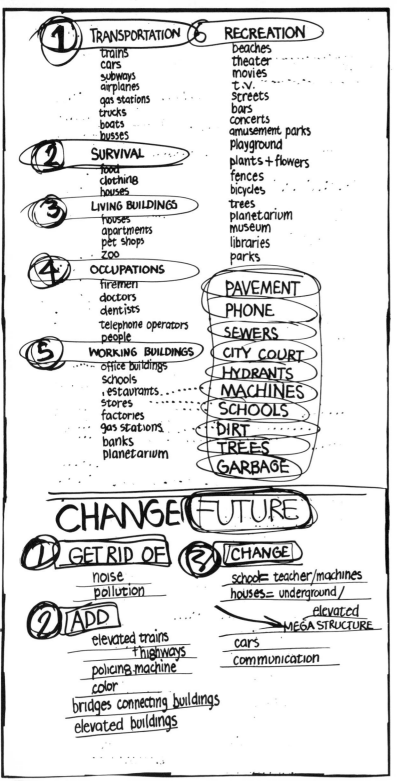

The essential ingredients of community scoring have been brought sharply into focus for me by the planning efforts of a class of seven- to eight-year old children at St. Ann Episcopal School, Brooklyn. The teacher (Eve Corey) has written a description of the "scoring" and the process. Intuitively the group started with (R) proceeded to score with (V) as feedback. The limitations of the medium are continuously apparent and much more determining in the performance than the limitations of the children.

"I first asked the class to name the different parts of the city. Then the class categorized the parts of the city that they had named. They began with the categories of food and shelter, which interested me, particularly to see that they had at their immediate disposal that basic classification. Then the problem arose as to how to define shelter. They realized that it was not just human shelter that they needed to deal with but other forms as well, i.e., the animals in the city. (On this point, the children also considered the need for benches to accommodate derelicts.)

"The class came into the new room and sat on the floor around four large pieces of cardboard, approximately 4' x 6' each, which were to be the base for the city. Throughout the planning, one boy had wanted to build subterranean houses. He asked how he could do it if the construction was going to take place on the floor. I realized then that I hadn't allowed for his project. He built some houses which were to be "imagined" as underground, but he lost interest and worked on above-ground houses. I now realize that my choice of rectangular

cardboards placed on the floor, which had been easy and convenient, created a limitation. As the students worked on the project they accepted the form of the ground that had been provided in setting up most aspects of the city, although, in one respect, the elevated train, they broke out of the bounds of the rectangle. This whole problem of what you're building on seems so clearly important after this initial exploration that I plan to begin with investigations of the land beneath when I work with this idea again."

—Eve Corey

But factors of Resource (R) analysis and good intention in community scoring are quite a different set of *ordering* principles than form-making. The tendency of many planners and architects to leap into the superimposition of form is crucial, even critical. The form, or better, the structure of communities for the future must emerge as a direct result of the

programmatic ideas set forward above, under Resources (R), and through the evolving scores of process. The "score" must not be a vehicle to arrive at a *particular* form, because we do not know and obviously never will know what the "ideal" form for community is. It is not the plan that is at stake, but the process of arriving at it.

Here, we begin to understand that the *plans* for communities are secondary to how they emerge. There are an infinite number of patterns possible—the variety of choices is almost endless. Each has some advantages and, inevitably, some disadvantages. No single pattern or configuration or structure will accomplish everything. But if we "score" the processes of community development, we have a much greater chance for success. We need to establish a scoring method which allows for lines-of-action which score in the implementation at each level, and allow for feedback and multivariable inputs, but not rigidity. Scores are an on-going process not a result.

Scores, then, should include every inventory item we can imagine. The process of inventorying is very significant to the score, since the score depends on these inventory items as source material. Both physical and human resources are to be understood and acknowledged *before* scoring begins. It cannot be overstated that inventory must include human inventory as well as physical and economic inventory for a community score to be valid. Community scores must rest squarely on ecological principles. They need to respect site, not only for its inherent structure and carrying capacity, but also for its environmental potentials—the *genius loci,* or the inherent qualities of a site. The score needs to include many technical items such as transportation mechanisms and other forms of communication among people and devices for freedom of action—but these technical items are not for their own sake. It needs to assume that inevitably there will be new technical devices of all kinds developed, which will supersede the old—in fact that change in "hardware" is inevitable, will continue, will develop, and perhaps even improve. What will not change, however, is the human basis for communities as the basic reason for building them. The microbiologist René Dubos has pointed out the unchanging nature of man's biological characteristics over many many centuries. "Cro-Magnon man," he says, "who lived as a hunter thirty thousand years ago . . . was probably indistinguishable from modern man mentally as well as biologically. He stood upright like us, had the same body shape, and his cranial size was at least as large as ours . . . the urges that shaped his familial activities and his tribal organization are still operative in us; his paintings, sculptures, and other artifacts

deeply move us, symbolically and aesthetically" ("Man Adapting: His Limitations and Potentialities," *Environment for Man,* William R. Ewald, editor).

Community scoring needs to enable all these processes to continue, to effect results to promote interaction and feedback, individual and collective input, and decision-making. It needs to function not only to guide process but to *make process visible.*

This is in direct contrast to the ruling-class principles that guided most ancient communities. In early days the priesthood held, closely guarded, the secrets of their craft so as to maintain power. They alone could influence deity and through deity the course of events. Secrecy *gave* power. Planning can also give power unless its processes are visible. The power inherent in secrecy, of course, has to do a great deal with the idea of withholding information. This can be caused by a lot of reasons. It may be a product of mistrust, of protection, of self-image, or of the fear of loss of control. It is much influenced by the artist-as-hero image. A very common reason is the fear that others, since they have little of the same background of experience, may put a different interpretation on facts or purposes than does a planner. The planner is therefore mistrustful of letting others choose between alternatives, because they might not choose the one he would like them to choose. This approach is endemic to statesmanship, and it operates often when science and politics implement or interface each other. A very common condition is to find political figures refusing to disclose information because it "jeopardizes national security." When wedded to military power, this withholding of alleged secret information allows decisions to be made based on privileged information not visible to the people, thereby granting unwarranted power to the holders of the information. This very same attitude was at the very heart of the early conflicts among scientists in the matter of the open or nonopen disclosure of atomic secrets.

The point I am trying to make here is that an essential ingredient in community scoring is to *make all the aspects of the score visible at all times.* If people are going to make errors in selections they must be allowed to do so within the scoring mechanism. A score treats people as adults, not children, and the scorer must abandon the idea of father-to-child relationships. This concept has as much to do with interpersonal relations or group relationships as it does with the planning of communities. If the scorer develops a closed, completely precise score, he then assumes complete responsibility. In the newer "open" scoring, members of the audience as well as performers often participate in performances. As a result they need to recognize that in these instances responsibility is shared by them.

The new scoring needs to be as visible as possible so as to scatter power, destroy secrecy, and involve everyone in the process of evolving their own communities. Power is a responsibility, so the audience as participator (that means *all* elements of society in the broadest sense), when given power, needs an understanding of what this means to itself as well as to the distributor of power. It is no easier to accept power and use it with responsibility and love than it is to relinquish it. There are all kinds of power, and motivation varies for each. There is leadership power, power for private gain, physical power, power given by the people to someone else to avoid their own responsibility. The whole crux of the power struggle has a great deal to do with the issue of "territoriality" as a biological phenomenon. In each of these instances power takes various forms. If you start a new community, power is evolved as part of performance (P). If a community exists, new entries have to grasp power or be given it by acknowledgment. The Berkeley People's Park was a struggle for power in which the owners saw no reason to give up territory and the "people" saw it as an attempt to exclude them from what they needed. It is often necessary to "take power" since it is so unwillingly and painfully given up. Out of this commitment came the slogan so typical of our time: Power to the People.

The new ruling class in the development of communities has been those who utilize land as a commodity for economic gain, the new entrepreneurs. These are the new breed of land-speculator developers who are the real architect-planner "scorers" of our environment. On the average they are venal, shortsighted, and their inputs into our community scores have resulted in disaster throughout America. They are largely responsible for the disintegration of the physical environment of our ghettos, for the appalling ugliness of urban and suburban sprawl. They have "scored" and misshaped most of our cities—interested only in the profit motive and the short-term profit motive at that. It is high time we demand to learn whether their decisions are the most valid ones for community action to base itself on. The artist-planner and the people are all at the mercy of the entrepreneur within the present context of our society. One of the benefits of visibility in scoring will be to make the functions and intentions of each recognizable and apparent to the other—to enable economics and economic gain (which are in themselves valid motivations in context) to be "scored in" to the process, and to become part of the artists' and citizens' recognized functions in dealing with community facts.

Equally important is the other side of the coin. Entrepreneurs can make valid and sociologically important community inputs. But many of their decisions for communities are based purely on short-term personal or corporate economic gain (a fact usually covered up by public-relations statements), and these are very often directly at cross-purposes with long-term community programs. The Sea Ranch, which shifted from excellent ecological criteria to short-range money grubbing criteria, is an unfortunate example. Whenever ecological scores are ignored private money is usually the reason.

A community has the right to make scoring decisions itself, based on its own understanding of the implications of action. The implication of this method of approaching planning through multivariable scoring systems is *not* to abrogate authority or decision-making in deference to chaos, or to avoid responsibility by making everyone responsible. What it proposes is a scoring process related to parts of the "systems approach" in operational research where all parts and participants, in the search for solutions to particular problems, have equal validity and strength in arriving at decisions. It is on this approach rather than a hierarchical structure of planning that the new scoring technique bases itself. This comes back full-cycle to our early discussion on scores in music and theatre, to the new attitude about involvement and against specialization. The new theatre, the new art, wishes once again to *involve* the people. In writing about The *5-Legged Stool,* I said: "Today's performing artist profoundly wants a partnership which will involve the audience as much as himself."

This conception means much more for us in the design and scoring of our communities than it does for the theatre. Cities themselves are beginning to be scored like theatre, in an intricate interrelationship between artists and communities.

SEPTEMBER 1970, conceived as a work of art, is the first attempt to use an entire city and its population as an art medium. It is a series of related urban events designed to deal with the city —specifically San Francisco—as a place of creation and involvement for its citizens and for a group of especially invited artists from all over the world who will design events using the city as their medium.

The period of SEPTEMBER 1970 will be thirty-five days in early autumn 1970 (August 30 — October 3). The place will be all of San Francisco, California.

SEPTEMBER 1970 will be an adventure for the people of the city and will seek to remove the boundaries between art, technology, and life. Through thirty-five uniquely designed days it will demonstrate how people, becoming involved both individually and together, can affect themselves, each other, and their urban environment.

The following score for SEPTEMBER 1970 is a non-verbal notational system. It illustrates how events and happenings can be designed into the city using a multi-dimensional system correlating time, space, people, and activities. The score is flexible and becomes fixed only at the points where the artist wishes it to. It places equal emphasis on all days and places within the city, giving artists freedom to establish their own focus within the score.

It is important to note that this scoring system is applicable to any other city, region, or environment, and any other time period because its methods and implications are universal.

THE DILEXI FOUNDATION
L. James Newman
Ralph Harper Silver

LAWRENCE HALPRIN & ASSOCIATES
Lawrence Halprin
Mike Doyle
Curtis Schreier

SEPTEMBER 1970

CITY-CALENDAR MATRIX

Events take place in areas of the grid that correspond to the day of the event.

The matrix recognizes that the city is made up of weekdays as well as weekends, and of typical places as well as special places.

Equal emphasis is given to all places and times leaving the individual and the artist to determine a focus.

An event on Friday, September 18th, would occur in the area of Potrero Hill. The artist could focus on a particular area and time within that framework (Jackson Park at 5 pm) or develop a series of events that would occur throughout the 24 hour period and involve everyone within the square mile area of September 18.

SCORE DEVELOPMENT   STEP 2

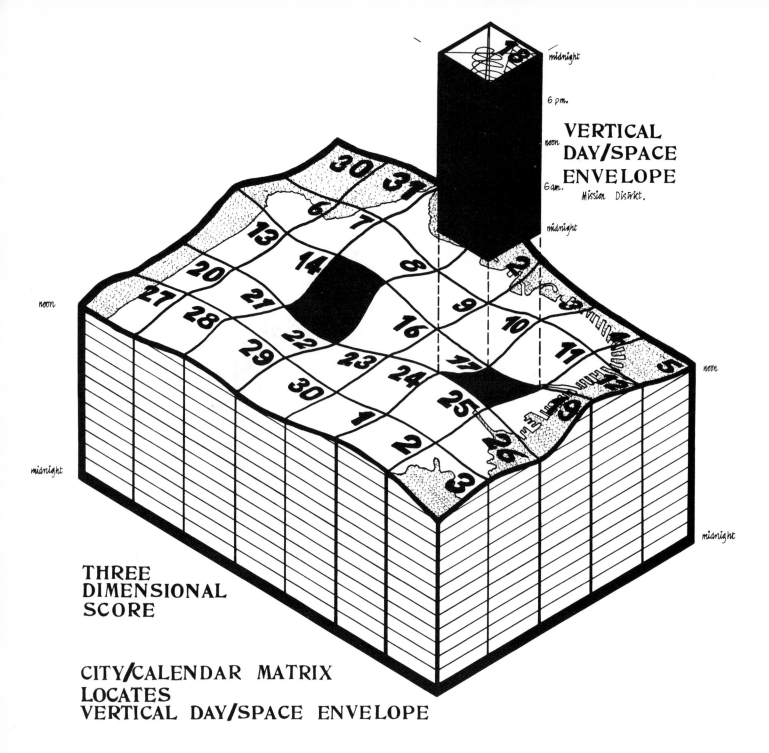

THREE
DIMENSIONAL
SCORE

VERTICAL
DAY/SPACE
ENVELOPE

Mission District.

CITY/CALENDAR MATRIX
LOCATES
VERTICAL DAY/SPACE ENVELOPE

SCORE DEVELOPMENT   STEP 3

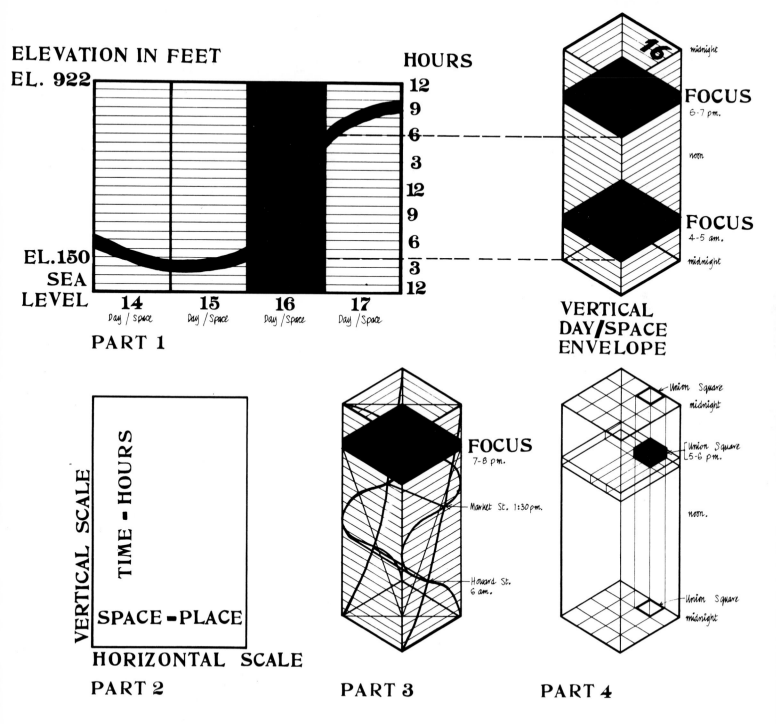

ELEVATION IN FEET
EL. 922

HOURS

EL.150
SEA
LEVEL

12
9
6
3
12
9
6
3
12

14   15   16   17
Day / Space   Day / Space   Day / Space   Day / Space

PART 1

16   midnight

FOCUS
6-7 pm.

noon

FOCUS
4-5 am.

midnight

VERTICAL
DAY/SPACE
ENVELOPE

VERTICAL SCALE

TIME - HOURS

SPACE - PLACE

HORIZONTAL SCALE

PART 2

FOCUS
7-8 pm.

Market St. 1:30pm.

Howard St.
6 am.

PART 3

Union Square
midnight

Union Square
5-6 pm.

noon.

Union Square
midnight

PART 4

SCORE DEVELOPMENT

STEP 4

© Dilexi Foundation and Lawrence Halprin & Associates, 1969

LEVEL ONE : THE GENERAL LEVEL

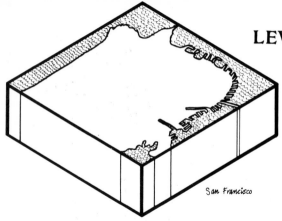

San Francisco

Level One will be the general level dealing with the entire city during the whole 35-day period. It will deal with typical activities during this period and activities planned through the Dilexi Foundation that will involve the whole city and its population.

LEVEL TWO: THE ARTIST'S LEVEL

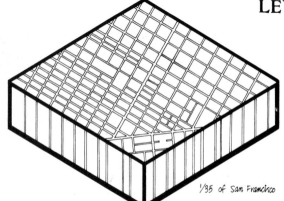

1/35 of San Francisco

Level Two will deal with the scores and events designed by individual artists for each of the 35 day/space envelopes. They will each be commissioned by the Dilexi Foundation to develop for a specific day/space envelope a score that will be their response to unique qualities of a particular time and place within the city.

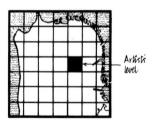

Artist's level

LEVEL THREE: THE COMMUNITY LEVEL

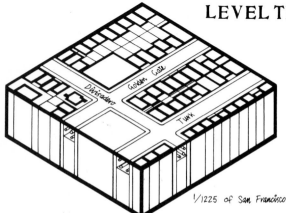

Divisadero   Golden Gate   Tunk

1/1225 of San Francisco

Level Three will deal with spaces within a day/space. It will deal with involvements in SEPTEMBER 1970 on an individual level. Any individual or group, a family, an office, a school, or a block in a neighborhood can develop scores or plan events (a silent dinner, a street fair, or a block party) for themselves or pick a score from a book of universal scores developed for this purpose.

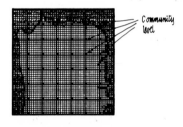

Community level

SCORE DEVELOPMENT

STEP 7

In September, 1969, one day of the score for September, 1970 was tried out in San Francisco to test community participation. The event was enthusiastically received.

This approach, of course, places great demands on the audience, the theatre audience, or the community-planning "audience," or the human-relationships "audience." If the audience wishes to become involved, there are consequences to this commitment. There are two sides to this relationship. The audience-as-community has an increased opportunity to affect what happens. This can be tremendously exciting and dynamic and far-reaching; but within the excitement there can be many failures and errors along the way. At the same time, this focuses a new series of demands on both the artist as scorer and the audience as community and participator. These new opportunities will lead to new results, to the degree that the audience members become responsive and enter into their role with energy, passion, and responsibility. It means that people can disclose information, respond with feeling states, reveal their needs, be alert to what is going on around them, and take on the role of active participants. The quality of the resultant experience depends in large measure on the ability of the artist to inspire and lead to peak experiences. On the other hand, for all members of the audience who want a "piece of the performance action" this also requires commitment to their own responsibility as participants. What happens is a mutual interdependence between artist-planner and audience in which each has his own role to play and both together form a work beyond the capacity of each individually. In helping to work within the planning process, the more the audience brings to the process, the more both the project and the people themselves benefit from this participation. There is no question that "involvement" can mean many things to many people. It can be, in fact, an excuse for license, for self-indulgence, for lack of program, for looseness in the evaluative mechanism. It can avoid the need for self-discipline and the acquisition of necessary knowledge and understanding in one's own field. It can allow for utter over-permissiveness. This attitude can become, in fact, a crashing bore in the performing arts. This is one of the dangers of continually using P rather than the whole RSVP cycle.

To differentiate between these roles demands much from the audience as well as from the artist. The audience, too, needs to know when it wants to be "used" or when the idea of involvement is simply a coverup for either ineptitude on the one hand or unwanted control on the other.

There is a mutual relationship and trust involved here between audience and artist that can be called ecological in the broadest sense of the term. If the true function of the artist is seen as an energy thrust which evokes the peak condition of awareness and output within the community, then he functions as an essential ingredient in an on-going energy chain, driving toward the highest potential of his ecological system. What we are describing here is a symbiotic rather than a parasitic relationship.

For the artist-planner this attitude and this approach is as demanding as for the audience. It implies that he is a "leader-member" of a team. Though more technically competent, his competence should enable him to guide, to show the consequences of actions, to inspire, rather than to decide by himself. One of the most vital functions the artist-planner can perform in the RSVP cycles is as a scorer (S) and performer (P). For it is in these two sections of the cycles that innovative work, thrusting toward new approaches unbound by the past, will be found. It is here, precisely, where irrational and intuitive drives will emerge unhampered by the important but limiting features of R, V in the cycle.

Architects have been exploring the idea of scoring without consciously using the term or the relationship of their concepts to open scoring in other fields. My friend Moshe Safdie, designer of Habitat, has sent me the following explanation of how he "scores" his architecture, using three-dimensional blocks from which any composition can be developed. This shows a remarkable similarity to the "cell-block" scoring method for *Parades and Changes.* In my view this is one of the most significant developments in the future design of our constructed environment. It is a way to score in an open way and allow for significant community involvement in actual performance. The same approach was used by Kenzo Tange in the design for modular swimming pavilions—even seating arrangements and aisle locations were to respond to the needs of audience.

Self-Composing Architecture. *"I approached the design of environment as design at two levels: one is to try to discover the inherent nature of the environment, and translate it to a building system, incorporating a geometric order which can be likened to a genetic code. The system is generated by functions and activities, by the resulting spaces, by services; it is expressed in elements which can be combined according to preconceived order and in conformity with a total structure. Once the system has been designed, it can be adapted to specific solutions; it composes its own space sequences.*

"After I designed the San Francisco State College Union, I adapted the total system to make a specific building, but I could have very well given this system to the students who would have adapted it themselves and made their own building. The general nature of the environment, the quality of spaces, of light, of movement would have been fundamentally the same.

"A generating system in environment, an environmental genetic code can be likened to a fugue. You design your basic theme or chord and determine the permutations and combinations by which it can be combined, within the laws of the counterpoint generating the fugue.

"I could have never designed the spacial sequences of Habitat; no one could have. I designed the basic system of modules, houses, and clusters, and the system in which they can be combined. These elements composed their own spacial sequences.

"This fundamental difference between composed and self-composing separates Habitat from the Western tradition of Renaissance Architecture. As a self-generating system, it is akin to the vernacular villages of Greece, Italy, or the Indian pueblos.

"These too, are building systems, environmental fugues, generating their own environment according to laws evolved by men over a great period of time.

"The contemporary vernacular will evolve as we discover the genetic codes of our cities."

—**Moshe Safdie**

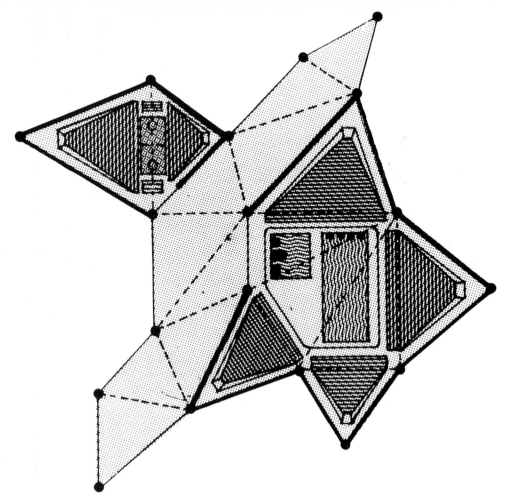

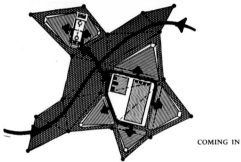

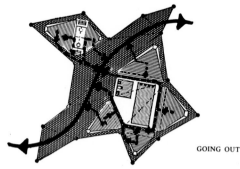

FUTURE GROWTH

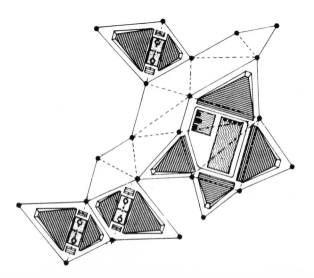

Kenzo Tange's thematic study of indoor swimming pool and gymnasium for the 1964 Olympics in Tokyo.

"Each triangular space of seats can be easily converted into an individual hall, thus getting six separate halls. The arena can be closed completely and serve for training with a minimum of maintenance expenses such as air-conditioning, lighting, and cleaning.

"The seating system provides maximum flexibility for the audience in the convenience of reaching their place and in leaving the hall. The system creates 'happened aisles' in all directions; aisles which are a result of the sequence and timing by which people happen to occupy their seats. Thus, the non-occupied seats create non-predictable aisles."

—I. M. Goodovitch, *Architecturology*

Within this approach the artist will have been charged with the responsibility of setting up all the inventories—ecological, social, humanistic, economic—and of inspiring creativity and then scoring them, but his will only be *one* of the inputs in the final process of playing the score. As one of the basic characteristics of scores, we have noted that no one person is more significant in a score than any other—all have equal weight and the importance of each is equal. It is while the score is being played that weightings based on ability or significance of ideas may emerge—not in the score itself. The difficulty is to keep *all* the options visible and to avoid hastily filtering some out even subconsciously. The R or V part of the cycles can outweigh S and P very easily at every step in the revolving cycles. This is difficult for the audience; often it will try to close down options too soon. I have heard it said by students of the creative process that creativity is the "ability to put off making decisions for as long as possible without becoming frantic." That is another way of saying: keep the RSVP cycles moving constantly.

This may be an appropriate place to comment on the new attitude toward participation. There is an increasing tendency to imply that participation in and of itself produces art. But it may not—this depends in very large measure on the artist himself. The role of the artist, as we have said, is to guide, inspire, drive toward peak experience, evoke creativity.

But I don't wish to confuse the reader about my own intentions. I do not mean momentary "grooving" or "turning-on" or "everyone expressing himself." All of these ecstatic states may be part of the creative experience, but they do not go far enough. The intention of audience participation will vary with the art form but it has a universal implication. In theatre it is to energize and reveal meaningful archetypal experiences. In community development it is to allow the people to develop their own community, their own neighborhoods, their own education, their own regions, so as to be congruent with their own lifestyle. It is a way for people to become *responsible* for what happens to them. Responsibility for one's actions is part of the implication of participation.

The artist has the demanding task of making the act of audience participation part of the art process—of making it deeply meaningful for the audience-as-community and at the same time a liberating force for the individual.

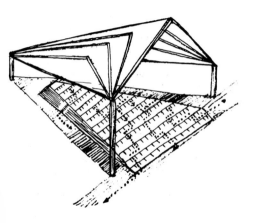

Frederiksted

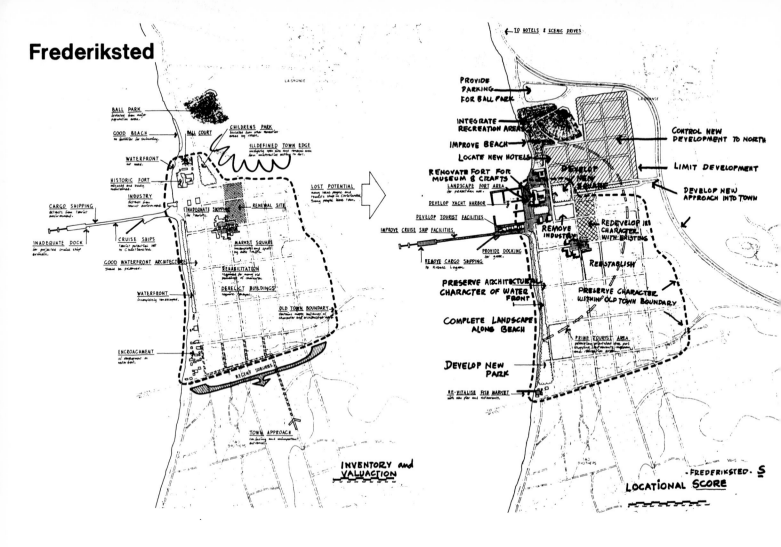

Fredricksted is one of the three original Danish towns in the Virgin Islands. In the present planning of this town for growth and change first came an analysis and inventory of Resources (R). The main Resources are the handsome picturesque qualities of the old architecture and its streets, the beautiful beaches along the waterfront and the tightly knit urban character. Valuaction (V) selects these as important to continue and preserve as against spreading suburban growth and/or destruction of the old Danish qualities. Then the locational Score (S) was developed indicating lines of action. The site plan is a further development of the score in which the scorer developed his idea of the graphic "quality" the town should have. It is a step toward Performance (P).

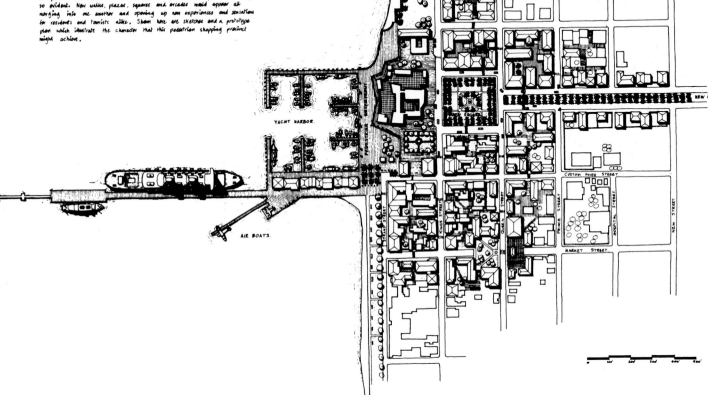

My office has been working in the Virgin Islands in this way, toward a series of island-wide community scores which are calculated to evidence the mutual influence of form upon density, density on transportation, acceptable population size on the other variables of open space, views, and so forth, as a multivariable scoring system to disclose options to all the community. Some of these scores follow and there are many others:

187

One of the most demanding parts of "playing the score" in community design is establishing value-systems and making value-decisions. The question, for example, arises constantly within communities: "Do we want this freeway?" And if we do, should it go via route 1 or route 2. Route 1 takes out fifty houses, two churches, and a school; route 2 destroys an important community park. Which shall we do? Or: perhaps we don't need the freeway after all or, more importantly, perhaps in our newer community we will design our living patterns so that freeways will not be necessary. This kind of value-question, complex as it is, is simple in view of many we face in the future.

The matter of value-systems has been given a great deal of attention with inconclusive results. Cost-benefit ratios are a very clear but myopic kind of value-system in which alternatives are rated by the number of dollars against arbitrary benefits accrued over say a twenty-year period. The closer this ratio approximates *one*, the closer to ideal it is thought to be. However this system of "Valuaction" (V) is adequate only for purely engineering-type structures, where subtleties of inquantifiable human behavioral or aesthetic values are not brought into the picture. As a scoring device it is completely inadequate. Perhaps the ultimate decisions that we can score into projects are multiplicity: that is, the larger the number of inputs, the more the score allows for a maximum of *real* interaction by many different people, the more "values" are expressed and then the more consensus will express the highest and best abilities and desires of the audience. Value in this sense is based on much more than nearsighted economic determinism but has to do with all the elements within the Gestalt of the culture. Thus it becomes ecologically-culturally sound.

One of the significant aspects of this kind of scoring is its emphasis on pluralism. In a pluralistic society *all* inputs of *all* people and all configurations of people have equal significance at the inception. In this it varies markedly from the "majority rules" kind of structure. In majority-dominated societies the feelings and desires of small groups are subordinated to what seems at a particular moment in time to be a general judgment of the majority of the people. This has obvious advantages over the dictatorship or king's "divine right" type of hierarchical system but still limits severely the ability of groups "less

than" the majority to do their own thing or affect their own input into a monolithic type of society. What is left is to give in, to cop out, or to try to change the status quo through revolutionary tactics. Student revolution, ghetto uprisings, alienation, draft-card burnings, protests of conservationists, all have much to do with the lack of cultural pluralisms and a feeling that alleged majority judgments are unjust. Any one of these alternatives seems less than a desirable mode of life. Even the "establishment" these days is being forced into taking revolutionary positions.

RICH BECOME RADICALS

San Francisco Chronicle,
Wednesday, September 3, 1969

The newly-radical rich are the privileged, upper-class people of Santa Barbara who have found that their established instruments of political power can't defeat the superior strength of the giant oil companies.

With their very own and very loyal legislators impotent at the doors of their very own White House, these Santa Barbarans have turned to direct action: sit-downs blocking oil trucks; yacht sail-ins circling off-shore wells; non-negotiable demands at City Hall; talk even of blowing up oil rigs with high explosives.

The January, 1969, eruption of oil through fissures in the subsea crust beneath a Union Oil Company off-shore well killed wild life for miles around, fouled beaches beneath the homes of Santa Barbara's most eminent citizens, and disrupted the local tourist industry. Oil continues to clump in dirty patches on the waters of the Santa Barbara channel today, despite the efforts of oil spokesmen and the Department of the Interior to minimize it.

The citizenry was increasingly outraged by the "all-powerful oil lobby"; increasingly disenchanted by legislators "in the pockets" of the oil companies; and disillusioned by scientists, "bought" by oil money, who tried to minimize the ecological damage that the citizens could see with their own eyes.

The oil-afflicted local citizens reared up and dramatized their fury by a series of demonstrations: pleasure boats picketed the Union Oil well; an ugly crowd of 500 influential citizens blocked a truck with their bodies; a hostile group of wealthy taxpayers shouted

epithets at Union Oil President Fred Hartley; a picket line was led by a highly conservative civic leader. There have been overt threats of violence—and the end, like the oil leak, is nowhere in sight.

The wealthy, the mature, the educated, and the conservative can all become radicals, too; all they need is an ox to be gored.

The American approach to consensus that was once thought to be a model for society may in fact be outmoded and require revision. It assumes majority "rule." But the presumed majorities on closer scrutiny often turn out to be establishment groups exercising an authority which was vested at some earlier time in a social system now noticeably irrelevant. The mere phrase "majority rules" begins to conjure up unpleasant images. We in America have always spoken of the "melting pot" where all differences were boiled down and diffused into the system, developing a kind of universal homogenous American "species." That seems now less and less wanted as an ideal. What seems more and more emergent is an ideal based on many variations of "species" each with its own lifestyle and habitat, if you wish, all living together in balance. That seems far more representative than some false drummed-up consensus. It is an ecological point of view leaking over into sociology, and it requires adequate political expression, if by political we mean the implementation of sociological-ecological needs.

This attitude requires (and it is beginning more and more to be demanded) that specific groups be allowed to do their own thing—within limits established through the score which are evolving and expanding—without either being swallowed up or put down. Other countries have for a long time found ways to accomplish this kind of pluralism. Americans have always looked smugly askance at political systems with many parties, but these *do* insure pluralism and the opportunity for many groups to exercise concerned interest. Politically, the pendulum has swung back and forth. The ideal, from a ruling clique's point of view, is no political deviation at all. That is pure Orwellism. Lacking that ideal the one-party system integrated with the state is as close as you can get; both communist and fascist countries have been organized under this system since World War I with varying degrees of success even from their own point of view.

The least ideal, from the point of view of efficient "ruling," is pluralism. It tends to be confused, nonlinear, difficult to administer, time and energy consuming, and difficult to control. But it is ecologically sound and insures as much as possible the opportunity for people to participate in the society in which they live—as active members of the whole RSVP cycles. It is the only way to insure diversity which has been shown to be not only sociologically desirable but also biologically necessary as well.

In scoring for groups, either as ephemeral entities or permanent organizations, I have found that the role of the individual self in the inner RSVP cycle is a major consideration. Often group-induced motivations are at variance with the real lifestyle and concerns of the particular individual, who inevitably pulls away from the score or resents it deeply. Often, too, group-induced motivations or demands induce a fantasy type of self-image where a person will fantasize about his own capabilities or attempt to fit other people's image of what he should do or be into other-oriented goals. It is kind of conscience-induced motivation, out of touch with reality and doomed to failure as part of the outer, community-oriented RSVP cycle. Conscience, according to Freud, is nothing but a fantasy, a continuation of the parents. I have found that there needs to be a congruence between the inner RSVP cycle of self and the outer group RSVP cycle for the two to function together well, as a basis for scoring for community.

What seems necessary is to find means to allow groups to have their own say and in fact affect decisions under which they will have to live; to live up to the idea of pluralism. In politics this is accomplished in different ways—for example proportional representation, or in the U.S. Senate filibuster, where an outraged minority can stall or forestall action. Although the image of the filibuster has been associated with the evils of discrimination, the principle is sound. In the systems approach to problem solving it is an accepted operating mechanism. In "scoring" it is a sine qua non of the whole idea. Pluralism as a method for involving people in the decisions by which they will live is essential to the idea of scoring of processes—of process as being the fundamental procedural base for an on-going society rather than results—no matter by whom determined. Thus the New England town

meeting may be a better ideal for tomorrow for most cities than the current model of representative democracy. Community scores depend on this idea and it forms, I believe, a valid basis for establishing value-systems within the community score idea. One of the major reasons for establishing the idea of process through scoring as the basis for a valid approach to community is the two-fold nature of communities and life relationships. On the one hand they are based on the biological fact of human permanence and man's unchanging fundamental traits; and in a behavioral sense his desire for permanence, security, and the status quo. On the other hand change and growth is the very essence of life and is evidence of a healthy person, his relationships to others, and indeed healthy communities. This is an ecological notion as well. Though systems get into balance there is change within the ecosystem at all times—there is a constant tension between stability and change.

Whether we agree with it philosophically or not we are faced in any event by change in technology which will not allow us to remain static. With each new modification in our technology—some of which become literally earthshaking—our community must react, must change. It is a concept which has its analogy in ecology: the idea of "disclimax." Disclimax prevents true climax in an ecosystem due to constant disturbance from outside such as fire, disease, or spread of artificially introduced species. We too as an earth ecosystem are, and will continue to be, I believe, in a continuous state of disclimax.

That is why process becomes so important. Due to the speed of change brought about by constant shifts in our technology, our planetary ecosystem can never really achieve a climax situation. It must always be slightly unbalanced. To constantly reconstitute a balanced situation as far as possible will remain our on-going biological, cultural, aesthetic, and ecological task for the foreseeable future. We will also quite clearly never know in advance what the cause of disclimax will be, what the new input into the system will consist of. Thus we cannot in advance of the fact either prevision what our community reaction will be or what form it must take. Any fixed diagram for a specific form or one or another solution will always elude the real issue.

For that reason we must establish a global mechanism to react creatively to the induced need for change. And that mechanism, I believe, is the deep understanding of process as a generator for solutions as basic to whole life-community on-goingness. Process as a mechanism for reacting creatively to the need for constant change through scoring gives us the needed vehicle for the future of communities.

Ultimately then the community score as a master score emerges as a personnel chart over time. It "scores in" the people who are to be involved in the process. And it discloses—perhaps—points at which configurations, conclusions, and dialogues must occur. I think perhaps it resembles the Minneapolis PERT chart, in its final form. But it has been backed up by many other scores each of which is as significant as the master score. These scores—the ecoscores, the transportation scores, the "happening scores," the poetry and music scores, the scores developed by all the minority groups in the community will all serve as major inputs for the total score which will be developed by the group established for this purpose. The score to be followed by the group of people who will develop the community score should emphasize these significant directions: (1) think about the effect of your actions on everyone else in the community, including the global community; (2) what you do is to be thought of as an on-going process; (3) try to keep as much flexibility in the score as possible so that it will admit of change over time; and (4) take into account the humanistic, biologic, and ecological implications of what you will do.

A Summary of the Characteristics of Scores

There is no one method of scoring. Scores symbolize processes and cannot be separated from the process itself. As scoring processes vary, and involve different persons, the scoring techniques, methods, motivations and performance resulting from them will vary. Scores are at the heart of the process of creativity.

Since there is no one possible accepted method of scoring (only *scores*) I cannot give you a manual on how to score. However, I have found that scores exhibit some *fundamental characteristics* that seem to be universal. Here are some of these characteristics:

1. For a score to function the participants in a score must exhibit a commitment to the idea of scoring and be willing to "go with" the specific score.

2. Scores themselves open up options rather than closing them down. As an example:
a. scores say "turn right," not "do not turn left."
b. they say "this area shall remain open" not "do not build here."
c. they say "I feel put down by that remark" not "you should not have made that remark." Wherever limitations exist they are under R or V in the cycle.

3. The way scores are presented has an enormous influence on the process itself and on the Performance (P). Nuances in scoring have great importance—often the scorer himself is not completely aware of how he is projecting himself and his own biases and preconceptions into the score. For example, here is a series of verbal scores which focus and define the quality and the nature of the experience:
a. On trip from San Francisco to Sea Ranch stop after one hour and observe.
b. On trip from San Francisco to Sea Ranch stop after one hour, interact with the environment.
c. On trip from San Francisco to Sea Ranch stop after one hour, graphically represent what you see.
d. On trip from San Francisco to Sea Ranch stop after one hour, wait until some event occurs in the environment which affects you.
e. On trip from San Francisco to Sea Ranch stop after one hour,
i. record what you see.
ii. record how you feel.
Each of these variations, though slight, would draw out marked differences in the Performance (P).

4. The element of *time* is always present in scores. Scores are not static; they extend over time.

5. Scores *themselves* are nonjudgmental. That is, they do not moralize or preconceive what is to happen. (Selectivity when it occurs is determined under a different element of the RSVP cycles [V] not in scores.) Scores tell what and why, not how.

6. Scores are non-hierarchical, that is, they treat all persons, groups, or elements involved

in the activity as having the same importance in the score. As the process proceeds, that is, the score is played, the "influence" of different inputs may be felt variously and weightings may change as activity continues, but the score itself does not preweight input. Scores are pluralistic.

7. Scores can be an end in themselves. They do not have to result in the process itself (which is another part of the RSVP cycles). Scores have a life of their own as distinguished from the Performance (P) of the score; for example, a plan for a building never built or a poem never read or a fantasy never lived out.

8. Scores relate very closely to natural processes since they are related to activity over time, are nonjudgmental, equalize input, and are nonresult-oriented.

9. Though scores themselves have the nonjudgmental qualities of natural systems they may be *used* for a variety of purposes and in many different contexts. To understand this configuration their relationship to the entire RSVP cycles must be understood clearly.

10. All parts of the score must be visible and clear at all times during the process. There cannot be secrets in scoring. This allows people to operate with a total view of the situation. Scores prevent "hidden agendas."

11. Scores can *energize* and *describe or control* processes. It is vital to determine *beforehand* which of these attitudes a score is going to express. Otherwise the participants will be confused about the expectation. In most scoring (as in most human relations) it is the confusion *between* these two attitudes that causes the focus of tensions and difficulty.

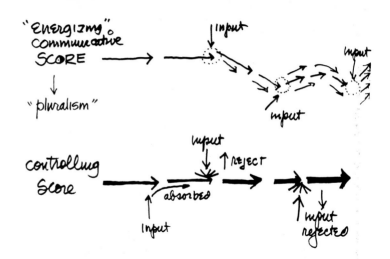

12. The question of whether scores energize or control depends on the relationship between scores and the other elements in the RSVP cycles. The elements of the cycle are as follows:

R   *Resource:* inventories resources, establishes motivations, enunciates purposes, determines requirements.

S   *Score:* describes processes leading to Performance.

V   *Valuaction:* incorporates change based on feedback and selectivity, including decisions.

P   *Performance:* establishes "style" of the accomplishment of the process.

There are many interrelationships and weightings of the cycle but the major configurations are as follows: these describe the intent of the relationship *during performance* (P), not during the scoring itself or what has led up to the score.

Relationships during Performance

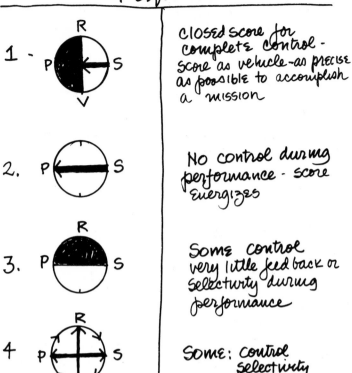

1. — **Closed score for complete control** — score as vehicle — as precise as possible to accomplish a mission

2. — **No control during performance** — score energizes

3. — **Some control** very little feedback or selectivity during performance

4. — **Some:** control selectivity feedback change growth

Under I. In the preceding chart the score is simply a vehicle to carry out the program as part of Resource (R), that is, the score and the program are really identical. There is no feedback, no chance desired or allowed, and the score must be as precise as possible—there is therefore no irrational input and *no art process involved.* This category is similar to the systems-engineering approach to problem solving.

Examples: Moon shot
Bank of America PERT chart
Bach musical score (differentiate
from Bach music)
Systems engineering

II. No programmatic (as part of Resource [R]) basis for scoring leaves a very close relationship between scoring and Performance (P). The Performance (P) evolves directly from the process which has been energized by the score. There is no selectivity except *during* Performance (P) by the persons involved and some selectivity established by the score itself. Such a relationship is exhibited by:

> Happenings
> New Music
> Driftwood Village event
> Ecological scores

NOTE: where only Performance (P) exists, without any score, what emerges is *improvisation.*

III. Where program as Resource (R) predates score and the two have sequential and equal weightings the Performance (P) reflects some selectivity and some control. The score has started from a basis established by the program and continues it in a creative way to energize processes. However, during Performance (P) very little or no Valuaction (V) occurs to influence the Performance (P) or the score as feedback. Such a score would be:

> Sports car rallye
> Football score
> Architectural scores

IV. The ideal relationship in complex situations exists when Valuaction (V) becomes part of the entire procedural pattern and is used as a feedback mechanism to encourage growth and change during Performance (P). Valuaction (V) is here meant as an observation of process as well as a judgment and oriented selectivity.

This relationship should ideally operate as the basis for:

Community planning
Theatre and other process-oriented arts
Community interactions
Personal interactions

This idealized relationship can be diagrammed this way:

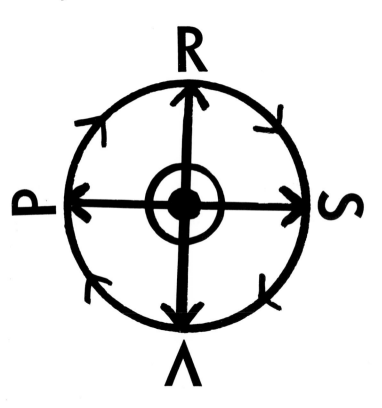

The ideal procedural relationships during performance in a multidisciplinary environmental event.

It is, of course, possible to bypass the "score" and proceed directly from Resource (R) to Performance (P) (with or without Valuaction [V]). Such a procedure leaves out the essential characteristics of the art process and *omits* creativity as a consciously organized process.

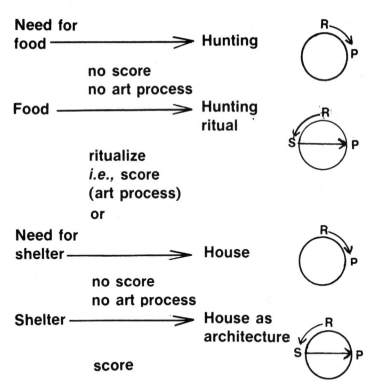

Need for
food ⟶ Hunting

no score
no art process

Food ⟶ Hunting
ritual

ritualize
i.e., score
(art process)
or

Need for
shelter ⟶ House

no score
no art process

Shelter ⟶ House as
architecture

score

In some ways this is the obverse of the pure Performance (P) situation which leaves out RSV and is simply then a matter of improvisation. The first leaves out creativity as a consciously organized process while improvisation (though creative) also omits the consciously organized process aspect of the creative act.

13. Scores (particularly open scores) allow for great personal leeway. They call for and encourage the highest creativity from *all* participants, since performance as a creative act emerges as the result of scores. For that reason each person involved in scoring will have very high demands placed on him, involving self-imposed discipline, craftsmanship, and acknowledgment of his relationship to others in the scoring process—all as an extension of his own creativity.

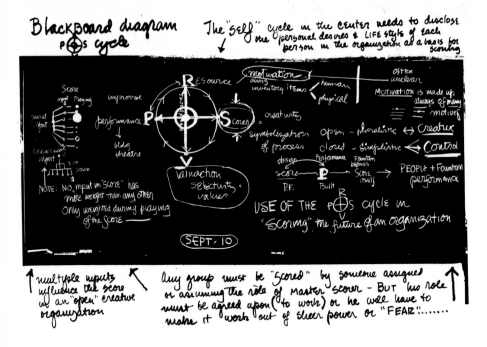

14. Dreams are like scores for an existential life-script. They are the most important and revealing kind of score for the psychologist to understand. Life itself is the Performance (P) of this existential score (Fritz Perls).

15. In addition to the applications indicated in the book, the RSVP cycles have potential in the following situations:

> Interpersonal behavior
> Group workshops
> Organizational charts for establishing
>> new processes and methods of
>> procedures
> Learning processes in all phases of
>> education and all age levels
> Structuring any group or organization as
>> well as artistic endeavors

For example, it is presently in use by the Dancers' Workshop Theatre as a guide in structuring a group that is living, working, organizing, teaching, and performing together.

The importance of pointing out the difference between "scores" and a system is basic to the idea of this book. A system is a closed and defined body with a beginning and an end. A system has a goal, and in order to achieve the goal establishes a specific way or technique of operation. A system is logical and sequential; it requires inputs but not feedback. A system implies order and regularity. A system relates things. A system starts with a preordained mission. There are systems to accomplish things; when things have gotten into good working order with everything functioning in a defined way they are called systems.

Scores have some characteristics of systems, but they differ profoundly. Scores are related to processes. Scores describe or initiate or energize processes. Scores include, in fact stimulate, elements of chance. Scores incorporate emotional states, include irrational elements. Scores require feedback as part of process. Scores are the essential ingredient of the creative process. Scores are not necessarily orderly, nor do they attempt to make things "function well." Scores are exploratory and not finite. Scores are open not closed. Scores help establish aims and motivation during scoring as part of process.

Systems, often, preamble scores. They can help factualize, inventory, give results of previous experience, store and evaluate knowledge. Scores, then, using the results of systems and including other inputs, guide the creative process.

Systems organize, scores guide. There may be "a particular system" for accomplishing a specific end or product. But let us not view any particular score as the only and ultimate solution in the creative process. Scores are a means of revealing alternatives, of disclosing latent possibilities and the potential for releasing total human resources. They are a way of inviting the unexpected; of expanding consciousness, encouraging spontaneity and interaction; in short the score is a way of allowing the creative process to be "natural."

In completing this book, I would like to make a few personal comments which seem to me important. All the scores and their processes which have been described here have had a very close tie to each other—a relationship—whatever the field they have been dealing with. They have all exhibited a quality of fantasy and of brilliantly irrational behavior and of considerable optimism about the future, with perhaps one or two specific exceptions. These scores are "hope-oriented." All have been trying to deal with the final issue of how, through art processes, man can enhance his ecological environment, which means: himself to himself, himself to where he lives, and himself to all the others living there; either momentarily as an ephemeral art event or through the permanent modification of the environment.

We are facing a period ahead when the very essence of our lives together will rest on how we deal with change in a positive and creative way. That is why we need new ways of looking at change: neither as good nor bad, not judged as to whether to allow or not allow, but ecologically, which means existentially. Change is going to *be.* Now how do we work with it?

All around us our structures are coming down around our ears. Our family structure is disintegrating, our political systems are falling apart, our accustomed moral structure is in question, our country is in a stupid and venal war, we are polluting our atmosphere, our land, and our water until it is only a matter of years before this planet will be unfit for human habitation. Worse, we are setting up divisions between our people which are forcing one side or the other to win, rather than allowing us all to gain. We are polarizing black and white, young people and adults, rich and poor, each lashing at the other, with the inevitable backlash resulting.

Just as severe as our eco-catastrophes are the other catastrophes latent in our society: we face social catastrophe, psychological catastrophe, personal catastrophe, national catastrophe, family catastrophe, community catastrophe. It is not enough to say this one or that one is at fault. We need creative mechanisms for change, based on aggregates of self-interest leading to community. We need a score.

There are, happily, evidences of attempts to deal with change creatively. Like it or not, most of these attempts lie among our young—our young people and our "young countries." There is clear evidence of a rejection of money grubbing and "thingism" as a motive in life among a large segment of affluent whites and a drive for part of the action among the blacks who have been denied it for so long. There is searching for expanded awareness of self, expanded families, and expanded groups. There are attempts at new forms of group living through "communes" into meaningful ways for people to live together, not only for specific goals but also for the *process* of living together.

Some of our most searing and urgent problems are going to be physical ones and the most urgent—the most critically urgent—of these is how to contain our population in order to make us congruent with our space and our resources on this planet Earth.

If we do not limit our numbers on earth by choice and decision, I am sure the normal ecological processes will do it for us, with unforeseen nonselective and very likely nonhuman-oriented results. We face communications problems and human relations problems and problems of equable distribution of the earth's bounty. Our "pecking order" is out of balance.

We have a long history behind us. I myself have just gotten back from a

working trip to Israel where everywhere I went thousands of years of human history lay beneath my feet. There one hears the echoes of past voices everywhere one goes, echoing in the streets or walking in the fields. Every stone has been walked on before, every cave inhabited. The scrolls are all around. The sky has been looked at by millions of eyes past, over the years, back to the early reaches of time. At the same time the *present* is active and full of problems. Some have been solved. Since the first time I was there, some thirty-five years ago, rocky desert landscapes, barren and hostile to man and animal, have been planted to seedlings which now have converted barren desert to fruitful habitats. Some of the seedlings I myself planted are today part of a forty-feet-high thriving forest, host to fox and wildflower, birds and wildlife. The voice of the turtle *is* heard now once again in a land which was sterile for years.

Just as ecological systems can be destroyed, they can be reconstituted, given love and care and motivation and the willingness to agree on all the aspects of the Score (S), the Performance (P), based on Resources (R) and Valuaction (V), and of course the dedication of people to accomplish all this performance as a life's work. If environment means that much, as it does in Israel, it *can* be reconstituted. Paradise *can* be regained.

But it must be regained (much better if it were preserved, as it should be in the United States) through group action, not through selfish means for private gain at the expense of the total environment—not one part for me and devil take the hindmost. Not: I will pull out of the land as much profit as I can, milk it dry and turn it over after it has been squeezed. That will leave us all the poorer. We need to find other criteria in the use of land. Why the system of private ownership of land as a commodity for speculation and gain is

acceptable to society is something I have never quite been able to grasp, on an ecologically ethical basis. It seems irrational.

F. R. Forsberg has stated very clearly the basic issue we all face ecologically—our willingness to see ourselves in a world view, not politically but as one single species.

(F. R. Forsberg, "The Preservation of Man's Environment," *The Subversive Science*, Paul Shepard and David McKinley, editors)

Perhaps the essential problem is that of man's ecological behavior. Most organisms occupy a very definite, usually rather restricted, position on a scale that ranges from the pioneer types who inhabit raw newly available habitats to the so-called "climax" organisms of mature stable communities. An important distinction separating these types is the duration of their occupancy of a habitat. The pioneer exerts a strong effect on its environment and tends to change it relatively rapidly, soon rendering it unsuitable for its own further occupancy. The climax organism, on the contrary, does not bring about or further such change, but lives in such adjustment with its environment that it is able to occupy it relatively permanently without serious modification. Indeed, such organisms may even tend to stabilize their environments and maintain equilibrium with them indefinitely.

. . . Man, as a species, has it within his power to fulfill the role of a pioneer, but in all probability a temporary, member of the world biotic community, on the one hand, or the role of a permanent climax species, preserving or even renewing his habitat and living in equilibrium with it, on the other.

. . . The enormous rise in incidence of insanity and less acute nervous, mental, and emotional disorders in the most

technologically advanced countries . . . It is entirely possible, even probable, that this is the modern form assumed by natural selection in the continued evolution of man . . . .

. . . Certain it is that to meet the strain of the new environment and the disappearance of the quiet and beauty of the old, man's nature will be changed. He will be harder, and the gentler traits that we now admire, as well as the appreciation of and need for the beauty of nature will be bred out of him.

Perhaps this is the real meaning of the revolution of today's young people against the "values" of the older generation. I think they see all this intuitively. Perhaps neither they nor anyone else for that matter understands quite clearly how to accomplish what is needed. But what they *do* know is that they do not wish to become harder or have love bred out of them. I hope that the RSVP cycles will help in their approach to life.

The future is an inconceivable conception. But I have felt that it was necessary to cope with it. I find it impossible and utterly fantastic to imagine what it will be like one thousand years from now with the rate of change increasing. But those of us dedicated to the celebration of life are searching for ways to support life processes and sustain this planet for its future inhabitants. What we do now, we know, will score the far future as well as the immediate future, which is tomorrow. Both futures are as important as the present for our children and all the inhabitants to be born around the world on this our planet Earth.

Ceremony of Us—a program by The Dancers' Workshop in collaboration with Studio Watts at the Mark Taper Theater, Los Angeles. A multiracial production in which the event was "scored" and, in a section of the program, the score is brought on stage and actively used in the choreography of the evening. Words in the score are pointed to in random order which activates the group to respond.

Illustrations

Photographs and drawings by Lawrence Halprin unless otherwise credited.

References

Alexander, Christopher. *Notes on the Synthesis of Form,* Harvard University Press (Cambridge, 1967).

Amirkhanian, Charles. "Applications of a Visual Transduction Notation System to Art and Life Experiences," *Folio KPFA* (Berkeley, California, 1969).

————. *Auto Blue Book Standard Touring Guide of America,* Automobile Blue Books, Inc. (New York, 1927).

Bacon, Edmund N. *Design of Cities,* Viking Press (New York, 1967).

Bihalji-Merin, Otto. *The World From Above,* Hill and Wang, Inc. (New York, 1967).

Blofeld, John, translator and editor. *I Ching; The Book of Change,* E. P. Dutton & Co., Inc., paperback edition (New York, 1965).

Bowers, Q. David; editor. *Guidebook of Automatic Musical Instruments,* Vol. I, Vestal Press (New York, 1967–68).

Cage, John. *Notations,* Something Else Press (New York, 1969). *Silence,* Wesleyan University Press (Middletown, Connecticut, 1961).

————. *Chinese Almanac,* Wing King Tong Co., Ltd. (Hong Kong, 1969).

————. *Climatic Summary of the United States,* Weather Bureau, U.S. Dept. of Agriculture (Washington, D.C.).

Darling, F. Fraser. "The Ecological Approach to the Social Sciences," in *The Subversive Science,* Paul Shepard and Daniel McKinley, editors; Houghton Mifflin Co. (Boston, 1969).

Darling, F. Fraser and John P. Milton, editors. *Future Environments of North America,* Natural History Press (Garden City, New York, 1966).

DeMars and Reay Architects. "Housing Study for New Town San Jose," mimeographed report, DeMars and Reay (Berkeley, California, 1965).

Doxiadis, Constantinos A. *Ekistics,* Oxford University Press (New York, 1968).

Eshkol, Noa and Abraham Wachmann. *Movement Notation,* Weidenfeld and Nicolson (London, 1958).

Farb, Peter *et al. Ecology,* Life Nature Library, Time Inc. (New York, 1963).

————. *Geologic Guidebook of the San Francisco Bay Counties,* Bulletin 154, California Division of Mines and Geology, Calif. Dept. of Natural Resources (San Francisco, 1951).

Giedion, Sigfried. *Space, Time and Architecture,* Harvard University Press, 5th edition (Cambridge, 1967).

Goodovitch, I. M. *Architecturology,* Ad Publishing Co. (Tel-Aviv, 1967).

Gray, Eden. *The Tarot Revealed,* Bell Publishing Co. (New York, 1960).

Gropius, Walter. *The Bauhaus: 1919-1928,* Charles T. Branford & Co. (Boston, 1959).

Halprin, Lawrence. *Cities,* Reinhold Publishing Co. (New York, 1963).

Halprin, Lawrence *et al. 5-Legged Stool,* Impulse (San Francisco, 1962), p. 37 ff.

————. *The Holy Bible,* King James Version, Collins' Clear-type Press (Great Britain).

Hutchinson, Ann. *Labanotation,* New Directions Book, James Laughlin (New York, 1954).

Jung, Carl G., *et al. Man and his Symbols,* Doubleday & Co. (New York, 1964).

Kadushin, Max. *Organic Thinking,* Jewish Theological Seminary of America (New York, 1938).

Kepes, Gyorgy. *Language of Vision,* Paul Theobald & Co. (Chicago, 1944).

Laney, Al. "The Talking Play," in *Fireside Book of Football,* by Jack Newcombe, Simon & Schuster (New York, 1964).

Lawrence Halprin & Associates. *Hennepin Avenue: An Urban Design Study for a Portion of Minneapolis, Minnesota,* mimeographed report, Lawrence Halprin & Assoc. (San Francisco, May, 1969). *New York New York,* Chapman Press (San Francisco, 1968). *Virgin Islands: Comprehensive Design Plan, Progress Report 4,* mimeographed report, Lawrence Halprin & Assoc. (San Francisco, 1968).

Leary, Timothy. *Interpersonal Diagnosis of Personality,* Ronald Press (New York, 1957).

Le Corbusier. *Oeuvre Complète 1952–1957,* George Wittenborn, Inc. (New York, 1957).

Lester, Gerald S., editor. *Baer's Agricultural Almanac,* Grosset and Dunlap (New York, 1969).

Market Street Joint Venture Architects. *Market Street Reconstruction: #3 Environmental Report,* mimeographed report, Market Street Joint Venture Architects (San Francisco, 1969).

McHarg, Ian L. *Design With Nature,* Natural History Press (New York, 1969).

McKinley, Daniel. "The New Mythology of 'Man in Nature,'" in *The Subversive Science,* Paul Shepard and Daniel McKinley, editors, Houghton Mifflin Co. (Boston, 1969).

Minneapolis Planning & Development Department. *Comprehensive Development Plan for Central Minneapolis,* Work Program and PERT Diagram, Minneapolis Planning & Development (rev. February 1969).

Moholy-Nagy, Laslo. *Vision in Motion,* Paul Theobald & Co. (Chicago, 1965).

Moholy-Nagy, Sibyl. *Matrix of Man,* Frederick A. Praeger (New York, 1968).

Müller, F. Max, editor. *The I Ching,* paperback, 2nd ed., trans. by James Legge, Dover Publications, Inc. (New York, 1963).

Mumford, Lewis. *The City in History,* Harcourt, Brace & World, Inc. (New York, 1961).

Odum, Eugene P. *Fundamentals of Ecology,* 2nd edition, W. B. Saunders Co. (Philadelphia, 1959).

Oosting, Henry J. *The Study of Plant Communities,* 2nd edition, W. H. Freeman & Co. (San Francisco, 1956).

Papus. *The Tarot of the Bohemians,* rev. ed., tr. by A. P. Morton, 4th printing, Arcanum (New York, 1967).

Perls, Frederick S., Ralph F. Hefferline, and Paul Goodman. *Gestalt Therapy,* 4th printing, Julian Press (New York, 1962).

Peterson, Roger Tory *et al. The Birds,* Life Nature Library, Time, Inc. (New York, 1963).

Portman, Adolf. *Animals As Social Beings,* tr. by Oliver Coburn, Viking Press (New York, 1961).

Rasmussen, Steen Eiler. *Experiencing Architecture,* M.I.T. Press (Cambridge, 1962).

Ricketts, Edward F., and Jack Calvin. *Between Pacific Tides,* 5th edition, rev. by Joel W. Hedgpeth, Stanford University Press (Stanford, Calif., 1952).

Ruesch, Jurgen and Weldon Kees. *Nonverbal Communication,* University of Calif. Press (Berkeley, 1956).

Sims, Agnes C. *San Cristobal Petroglyphs,* Southwest Editions (Santa Fe, New Mexico, 1950).

Siu, R. G. H. *The Man of Many Qualities: A Legacy of the I Ching,* M.I.T. Press (Cambridge, 1968).

————. *Source; Music of the Avant Garde,* issues nos. 4 & 5, Vol. 2, No. 2, and Vol. 3, No. 1, Composer/Performer (Davis, Calif., July 1968 and January 1969).

Spiller, Jürg, editor, *Paul Klee: The Thinking Eye,* tr. by Ralph Manheim, George Wittenborn, Inc. (New York, 1961).

Thomas, William L., Jr. *Man's Role in Changing the Face of the Earth,* University of Chicago Press (Chicago, 1956).

Tunnard, Christopher. *Gardens in the Modern Landscape,* Scribner & Sons (New York, 1948).

Tunnard, Christopher and Boris Pushkarev. *Man-Made America: Chaos or Control?,* Yale University Press (New Haven, 1963).

Wheat, Joe Ben. "A Paleo-Indian Bison Kill," *Scientific American,* Vol. 216, No. 1, pp. 44–52 (January, 1967.)

White, Lynn, Jr. "The Historical Roots of Our Ecological Crisis," in *The Subversive Science,* Paul Shepard and Daniel McKinley, editors, Houghton Mifflin Co. (Boston, 1969).

Williams, Emmett, editor. *An Anthology of Concrete Poetry;* paperback edition, Something Else Press (New York, 1967).

Wyman, Leland C., editor. *Beautyway: A Navaho Ceremonial,* Bollingen Series LIII, Pantheon Books (New York, 1957).